450

THE
EYE
OF
HISTORY

*The Motion Picture
from Magic Lantern to Sound Film*

The camera is the eye of history.

—Mathew B. Brady (1822-1896)

The combination of such an instrument [Edison's Kinetoscope] with the phonograph has not . . . been satisfactorily accomplished; there can, however, be but little doubt that in the . . . future . . . an entire opera, with the gestures, facial expressions, and songs of the performers, with all the accompanying music, will be recorded and reproduced by an apparatus, . . . for the instruction or entertainment of an audience . . . ; and if the photographs . . . have been made stereoscopically, and . . . each series be independently and synchronously projected on a screen, a perfectly realistic imitation of the original performance will be seen, in the apparent "round," by the use of properly constructed binocular glasses.

—Eadweard Muybridge (1830-1904)
*in the preface (dated December 1898)
to his book entitled* Animals in Motion, *published in 1899*

I believe, as I have always believed, that you control the most powerful instrument in the world for good or evil. . . . Remember that you are servants of the public, and never let a desire for money or power prevent you from giving to the public the best work of which you are capable. It is not the quantity of riches that counts; it's the quality which produces happiness, where that is possible. I . . . wish you a prosperous, useful, and honorable future.

—Thomas A. Edison (1847-1931)
to representatives of the motion-picture industry assembled to honor him on his birthday in 1924

THE
EYE
OF
HISTORY

The Motion Picture
from Magic Lantern to Sound Film

BY JULIUS PFRAGNER

Translated and adapted from the German
by Theodore McClintock

 RAND McNALLY & COMPANY
Chicago • New York • San Francisco

Translated from *Kino, der Roman einer Erfindung*
Copyright 1958 by Verlag für Jugend und Volk, Vienna

CONTENTS

PREFACE

Many men have contributed to the development of photography and the motion picture: opticians, painters, mathematicians, physicists, chemists, inventors, industrialists, and men who can only be called amateurs. The author of this book, in telling the story of their achievements, emphasizes the work of the pioneers who made the decisive inventions. The story covers more than a hundred years, and the chosen pioneers lived in half a dozen countries.

To give us a vivid picture of the background against which those pioneers worked, to concentrate scattered events within compact scenes, and to maintain narrative continuity through the course of this long and wide-ranging story, the author has introduced a few fictional characters. Such characters are never given credit for any of the achievements of the pioneers, and their conversation, though it is, of course, fictional, does not give us false information about the subject of this book. In short, the history of photography presented here is, I believe, authentic.

The reader can easily find out whether a certain character represents a real person, for all real persons, with a few exceptions, are entered in the index. The exceptions are relatives, friends, and minor assistants of the pioneers—people who did not themselves participate in the development of photography. The reader, if he really cares, will have no trouble recognizing such people. Simon Stampfer (Chapter 2) no doubt had a laboratory assistant, whose name may well have been Frutschnigg; Franz Uchatius (Chapter 5) was married, and his wife was no doubt named Anna; the Grand Café in Paris (Chapter 10) no doubt had a manager, and his name may have been Carnot. Seeing no reason for entering the names of the assistant, the wife, and the manager, I have omitted them and other such names, along with the names of the few characters that I feel sure are fictional, from the index.

That index, besides serving the usual purpose of an index, offers several kinds of additional information: biographical and historical details, definitions of technical terms, descriptions and illustrations of historically important apparatus.

It was not always easy to dig out the biographical and technical information that the reader will find there. For help in that effort I am grateful to Denis Courtney and other members of the staff of the Society of Motion Picture and Television Engineers.

—THE TRANSLATOR

1.

AN OPTICIAN LOOKS FOR WORK

"DOES the shadow bother you?" Helpfully the student moved a massive telescope tripod to one side.

"Shadows have never bothered me, Student Luser," answered the optician, as he stood up to his full height. "As Privy Councilor Goethe says, 'where much light is, there is deep shadow.' Since I make my living by light, I must take the shadows too." Johann Friedrich Voigtländer bent again over the microscope, adjusted the tube by turning a large knurled screwhead, and carefully swung the little mirror under the stage into another position.

Luser's eyes, which always seemed to be laughing, wandered around the dusky room. Why, he wondered, had the old man invited him into this inner sanctum, which was cluttered with optical apparatus of every kind? Even the walls were covered with precise drawings that exhibited the paths of light rays through telescopes, microscopes, single lenses, and combinations of lenses.

Dully, through a low door, came the noise of the workshop: the grinding of eyeglasses, the humming of lathes, the chatter of journeymen. One of these was whistling a song,

"Am Brunnen vor dem Tore, da steht ein Lindenbaum," which the student recognized at once. It was by that composer, named Schubert, who lived, as Luser did, in a little suburb outside one of the old town gates. Luser often encountered him in the evening, when he called for Miss Agatha.

"To come back to this microscope, Student Luser," said Voigtländer, a stocky man who looked as if he always knew exactly what he wanted, "it is, as you can see for yourself, an old model. It's not the best I have made, but to a student it will still be useful. I'm glad to let you have it—gratis, of course."

Luser's chubby face beamed. "Why, that's very kind of you, Mr. Voigtländer."

"Now, now—I am not so generous as you think. I hope, you see, that you can do me a little service in return, and that is why I wanted to talk to you." He sat down, leaned back comfortably, and paused as if he wanted to heighten Luser's suspense. "You really love optics, as I noticed a long time ago, and you are always there at the university, listening to lectures. And so, it seems to me, you are the right man for what I want. Will you keep your ears open so that you can give me hints for my work—suggestions—new ideas . . .?"

A shadow of doubt passed over the student's baby-like face. He began cautiously: "If I understand you rightly, Mr. Voigtländer . . ."

"You will understand me rightly only when you know what has led up to my proposal. When my father opened his workshop here in Vienna, he produced little more than compasses for schoolmasters and scholars. That didn't satisfy him; so he sent me to London, where I learned to grind first-class lenses under one of the best men in the trade. Along with that I managed to find out—without his knowing—how Wollaston made his periscopic eyeglasses. You know them, the meniscus lenses through which you can see clearly, not just what is in front of you, but what is off to the side. Later I introduced these glasses into Austria and Germany—a great success, even in a business way!"

His look of pride held Luser's attention for a moment. Then he continued: "And three years ago—yes, it was in 1823—I had another success, my telescope. Stampfer—Simon Stampfer, professor at the Technical College—helped me with the calculations." Voigtländer snorted through his bushy beard. "Since then, Student Luser, I have felt sure that it would pay to keep a sharp eye on these learned gentlemen. Apparently, under all their scientific gibberish, they sometimes turn up a bit of knowledge that an able craftsman can use—for the benefit of mankind and to his own advantage."

Luser knew that he should respond to this remark; but, embarrassed, he played with the lens he was holding between thumb and index finger and did his best to avoid meeting the optician's eye. The journeyman in the workshop was warbling *"Horch, horch, die Lerch' im Aetherblau."* Luser knew this song too. He had been in a beer garden when Franz Schubert composed it there. When it was finished, everybody in the garden had joined in singing it. It had been a wonderful evening.

"That's my boy, Friedrich, singing in there," said Voigtländer. "Fourteen years old today! He works at the lens-grinding machine. How long will it be, I wonder, before he's on his own? Will he, I wonder, ever look down his nose at his father, who, at forty-seven, got stuck in a dreadful rut making eyeglasses?"

Luser knew no way to answer this. He spoke slowly, hesitating: "It isn't that . . ."

But Voigtländer interrupted him angrily: "Sir, listen to me! Progress is being made in all departments of human life: in agriculture and in mining, in textile manufacturing and in the iron industry. The steam engine has revolutionized production. Millions are now being made with illuminating gas and with other chemical products. Only in optics is there no change, absolutely none! We still look piously through Janssen's microscope and Kepler's telescope—as we did two centuries ago. What's the matter with your science, sir?"

Luser was no longer embarrassed. "When I think about the lectures I hear, such as those given by Professor Ettingshausen, I see no possibility of finding any practical application in them. What can you do with diffraction, interference, double refraction, and polarization?"

Voigtländer held his hands over his ears. "Interference! Polarization! No, no, they mean nothing to me. Think of something simple, something like the periscopic eyeglasses. What was so special about them? Ground convex on one side, concave on the other! That's all! But think how many people they've made life easier for! And now I ask you, is optics good only for helping bad eyes, for helping sick people? Can't it do something for healthy people too—for everybody? Something that would benefit all of us or give us all pleasure?"

Luser's chubby face suddenly beamed again. "How about the magic lantern? Think of something to do with that!"

"The magic lantern?" Voigtländer's surprise turned sharply to sarcasm. "Why, Student Luser! The magic lantern is nothing but a combination of the camera obscura and mirror-writing. Leonardo da Vinci knew the camera obscura —perhaps invented it—more than three centuries ago! Mirror-writing was known in ancient times! And the magic lantern was described in print at least two hundred years ago! I congratulate you on your 'modern' idea, but I don't believe it's worth this microscope."

The student, to Voigtländer's surprise, did not back down. "Think a moment," he said. "What does a magic lantern consist of?" He paused to rehearse his facts. "There is a concave mirror behind the lamp, isn't there, which gathers the light and reflects it through the slide? The light rays cross in the little opening at the front of the case. And what is there in front of the case? The tube containing the lens, which throws an enlarged picture on the screen. Concave mirror, case, slide, lens—put them together, and you have work for a capable optician. Work—and profit!"

"Work, certainly, but profit? Who is interested nowadays in a magic lantern?"

Then Luser played his trump. "Mr. Voigtländer, not long ago, with my betrothed, Agatha, I saw a magic-lantern exhibition—or performance—whatever you want to call it. It was in a tent. You have no idea how people crowded in to see it! The operators of such shows are not satisfied, of course, with exhibiting pleasant and innocent scenes. They give us blood-dripping tyrants, repulsive idols, monsters . . . and always the devil, complete with fur, horns, tail, and stuck-out tongue. All magic-lantern pictures!"

"And people go to look at such things?"

"See for yourself! Just come with me to the Prater some day."

They met on a bright Sunday in May. The optician had put on his best dress-coat and the student his gayest expression in order not to look out of place in the merry crowd that sauntered with them across the Danube Canal and into the Prater.

Voigtländer was amazed at the number of strollers.

"Yes," said Luser, "all Vienna comes here when the weather is inviting. In the thirty years since the Emperor threw the Prater open to the public it has become the place where we all go for a good time, no matter what our tastes are. But in forty-seven years you have not become a real Viennese, Mr. Voigtländer!"

"That I should not like to admit," said the optician stiffly. "But it's true that I'm always in my workshop. Perhaps that has made me unworldly."

The student showed him where the stately public garden lay and where they had to turn off toward the amusement park.

"And where are the magic-lantern pictures shown?" Even the most magnificent spring day could not distract Voigtländer from his purpose.

They wandered among jerry-built sheds, where enterprise and ingenuity enticed the sensation-hungry crowd of sightseers with fire-eaters, sword-swallowers, dancing bears, and bowling alleys.

Luser would have liked to stop at the shooting gallery. The attendant, who had just sent a leaden bird flying along the cord toward the circular target, got ready to send another one.

But Voigtländer was inflexible: "And the magic lantern?"

The student sighed and went on. Behind one of the new merry-go-rounds they found two showmen who had set up their magic boxes on little carts and, for a kreuzer, allowed the curious to take a look through the peepholes. The monotonously chanted descriptions of the pictures to be seen there made Voigtländer turn up his nose. He was about to vent his disgust in a juicy bit of insolence when Luser exclaimed, "There is our man!"

The student drew the optician to a shed, in front of which, on a beer keg, stood a tall, haggard man wearing a sloppily tied neckerchief. This fellow had already yelled himself hoarse, but he went right on: "You will see here, ladies and gentlemen, things you have never seen before: phantasmagorias, my unique phantasmagorias! My art will reveal to you things you could never even imagine: terror, awe, horror will make your flesh creep! Enter!" They got into line at the entrance. Voigtländer was amazed at the number of people who waited patiently until, one after another, they could pay their twenty kreuzers to get in.

"You can't say the fellow is cheap!" he grumbled as he squeezed through the doorway.

"He's found out exactly how much he can make out of an idler's appetite for thrills," answered Luser.

They found themselves standing in a meagerly lighted

room. Voigtländer, after his eyes slowly adapted themselves to the mystic twilight, burst out reproachfully: "What's all this stuff? Nothing but skulls, bones, weathered gravestones."

"This is just a prelude—to put us into the right mood," explained Luser with a grin.

The first magic-lantern picture suddenly appeared on the screen at the front of the shed. The hoarse voice of the fellow with the badly tied neckerchief commented on the pictures, each more gruesome than the one before. At the end, while death-bells tolled and a storm lashed the screen, Death himself bore down on the spectators. People squealed, shrieked, screamed, and a woman beside Voigtländer fainted.

"And that is supposed to provide work for an honest optician?" grumbled Voigtländer as soon as they were out in the open.

For Luser, after what he had just experienced, it was hard to think of a good answer to this question. "I often ask myself what drives people into such places," he finally said. "I suppose it's simply curiosity, the desire to see, to watch things happen, which man is apparently born with. That desire was what drove the people of ancient Rome to the circus and to the great religious festivals. And—it has just occurred to me—weren't those festivals always held in caves, in dark rooms? Why? Perhaps the bright picture in a darkened room has a special power to attract us."

Voigtländer wanted to say something, but the student didn't give him a chance.

"First answer a question. Were you ever in a completely dark room in which a little stump of a candle was burning? You were? Then you know what a magical power that flickering light has! Maybe the people in that shed are attracted by the same magic. What do you think?"

The optician lost his patience. "What if they are? What do I care? I'm looking for work, work for my hands!"

His vehemence did not disturb the student. "I'm coming to that, Master! We agree, don't we, that we can count on human curiosity, the desire to see? Well, then, how do we know that people would not like better pictures even better? Maybe we simply have to give them a chance to see better pictures. I think I know a way to do that, and it's a way that you will be interested in."

He stopped, shuffled about hesitantly, plucked childishly at Voigtländer's snow-white cravat, then pulled himself together. "To tell the truth, I have a confession to make to you, Mr. Voigtländer. Not long ago you gave me a microscope. That was very good of you, and I really need it. But do you know, Mr. Voigtländer, how you could have given me a much greater pleasure?" He looked expectantly at his companion, but Voigtländer did not know how to answer. "With a camera obscura!" continued Luser. "I have wanted one since I was a child. And for this reason: I always wanted to draw, to make and keep pictures of my surroundings. But I have no talent at all! Still, I told myself, if I had a camera obscura, with a flawless converging lens at the front, I could stretch translucent paper across the back, where the inverted image appears, and draw the outlines. In that way even a bungler like me could make true-to-nature pictures."

"And the magic lantern?" The optician's curiosity showed through his brusqueness.

"In a moment! Such cameras, easily handled, equipped with certain ingenious devices—wouldn't they make work for you? Just think of all the untalented people who would like to draw! But there's something even more important! Don't you think that people would get much more pleasure out of looking at their pictures if they could project them onto the wall with a magic lantern? Well? Now you have to admit I've got something! And just imagine the crowds that would come to see a series of such pictures from strange, distant lands!"

Voigtländer held his head in his hands. "Student Luser! You seem to be living in Cloud Cuckoo Land! Your dreams are remarkable, but I can't live on them. You are a fool . . ."

Luser didn't hear the rest of his unflattering remarks. With emphatic deference he sprang to one side in order to make way for two gentlemen who, apparently coming from the public garden, were walking toward the city. The elegantly dressed civilian acknowledged Luser's greeting with a curt nod, but he remained attentive to the officer at his side, who was talking to him with noticeable urgency.

"That's Ettingshausen," the student whispered to his companion, "Professor of Physics at the University of Vienna." Voigtländer also lifted his hat.

"And that," said the officer, as the two men passed Voigtländer and Luser, "is why no one can argue me out of my conviction that optics, today, is one of the most fascinating fields of work and that it may be preparing the greatest surprises for us."

Ettingshausen stopped a moment and looked at the officer. "If the series of experiments that I am now performing give the results I expect—well, I may come to agree with you, Major Hauslaab." Then the two went on.

Voigtländer could see this Major Hauslaab turn eagerly to Professor Ettingshausen as he said, "Then I'll call on you again, Professor. I can hardly wait to hear what . . ." Strollers moved in behind the two gentlemen, and Voigtländer heard no more. He still stared in their direction, hardly hearing, at first, what Luser was saying to him: "Ettingshausen is already a little conceited—a bit proud, perhaps, of having been called so young from Heidelberg to Innsbruck and then to Vienna. Anyone who knew him . . ."

"But you know him, you know him well?"

Luser had no idea that this question was the end of a series of thoughts that were not exactly flattering to him. Why, the optician had asked himself, do I bother with this dreamer, this visionary, when I may be able to talk to a real expert? This Major Hauslaab goes to see the Professor! And what he can do . . .

Now it was the optician who seized the student by the

cravat. "I make you a special and surprising offer, Mr. Student. If you can arrange for me a conversation with Professor Ettingshausen, you will receive the camera obscura you have wanted so long."

"What is light?"

Andreas Ettingshausen, standing before his seated visitors in his faultlessly tailored coat, which emphasized, by its high collar, his elegantly sloping shoulders, paused for reflection, as if to survey the full meaning of his question; and then his glance wandered from the student, who was smiling with embarrassment, to the optician, who met his look with self-assurance.

"For me, Mr. Voigtländer," he said, in the manner of a lecturer, "light consists, as in Newton's theory, of minute particles of the finest matter, which are different for each color and which proceed from the source in all directions with a speed of 300,000 kilometers a second. Huygens, on the contrary, maintained the wave theory: that light is not matter but a *condition* of matter—a condition that consists of extremely rapid vibrations. Huygens, to be sure, found himself forced to assume, as the executant of these vibrations, a weightless stuff, the luminiferous ether, which fills the whole universe. The vibrations of this ether produce sensations of light in the eye, just as vibrations of the air produce sensations of sound in the ear. Such light vibrations would, it is true, have to be transverse—that is, perpendicular to the direction of propagation of the light; and that fact, if we trust the laws of mechanics and the theory of elasticity, is not easy to reconcile with the assumption of the luminiferous ether. That is my world, Mr. Voigtländer. Can you do anything with it?"

Voigtländer spread his fingers out on his knees and looked at them searchingly and reflectively as if he had nothing to think about at the moment except how those two hands, which were clearly those of a handicraftsman, could have strayed into these surroundings. Since he did not answer, Ettingshausen went on: "And, conversely, I can do nothing with your world, in which the camera obscura and magic-lantern pictures seem to play a special role, as Mr. Luser mentioned at the beginning. Such things are, unfortunately, considered a part of optics, although, far removed from our scientific deliberations, they pursue their not exactly brilliant or honorable career at amusement parks, fair grounds, and church festivals—and are designed, for the most part, to satisfy the common people's greed for sensations."

Neither of the two visitors took advantage of the painfully oppressive silence. They sat with their heads down as Ettingshausen's glance passed over them slowly and haughtily.

"The only way I could help you," said the Professor condescendingly, "would be by ordering, as occasion required, a well-ground lens. Perhaps, for this purpose, you will leave your name and address here."

Voigtländer was so vexed with himself that he was not capable of orderly thought, and almost mechanically he scribbled his name and address on a slip of paper. Then he stood up and walked heavily and awkwardly to the Professor. "I also recommend myself for special jobs."

Perhaps, at that moment, Ettingshausen realized how disappointed the man was and felt some sympathy for him. He turned directly to the student: "Or am I wrong? Can you offer some encouragement to the Master Optician?"

Luser stood up as if pulled out of his chair. "No, no! I am entirely of your opinion, Professor!" Then, because Voigtländer gave him a look of unconcealed scorn, he added, uncertainly, in a constrained and embarrassed tone: "We only thought . . . because light . . . well, plays a special role in life . . ."

Ettingshausen interrupted him coolly and sharply: "Student Luser! The special role of light, as you call it, can be traced back to the world of sagas and fables, of the mystical, and it no doubt originated in the traditional doctrine, found in every religion, that a god gave men light. But scientific theory . . ."

He had to stop, for the pounding on the door was too loud. The pounding stopped, the door flew open, and Spannagel, the janitor, his face red, rushed in. To Ettingshausen's amazement he didn't even try to draw himself up in his usual correct and rigid attitude; he simply burst out with his news: "Mr. Professor! A son has just opened his eyes to the light of the world! Congratulations!"

The two visitors suddenly found themselves alone in the room.

Then Luser relaxed from his rigid attitude and turned to Johann Friedrich Voigtländer: "Spannagel should have said, to be exact: 'A son has opened his eyes to the transverse vibrations of that luminiferous ether that we don't really know what to do with.' "

The optician turned slowly and carefully, as if he were a bomb that might explode. "Young fellow," he said at last, "you have earned your camera obscura—and also my contempt."

And then Luser was alone.

2.

A WORLD-SHAKING PLAYTHING

THE coachman cracked his whip encouragingly. The two white horses neighed playfully as if they knew that they were hauling the merry passengers to one of the rustic taverns that line the Vienna Woods.

It was the ingenuous silk-weaver with the copper-red nose who first noticed the extraordinary figure in the vineyard they were passing. "There, look!" he shouted. His fleshy hand pointed to a worthy gentleman in a black dress-coat, who, on the other side of the picket fence, was running along with the carriage.

"I know him!" roared the man sitting opposite. "I saw him last week on another road. He always runs along beside a moving carriage. Otherwise he seems to be a genteel sort."

"Wouldn't you rather use the road?" called the silk-weaver to the stranger. The whole coach shook with laughter. Only Laboratory Assistant Frutschnigg remained quiet. He had chosen the last seat so that he could stretch his wooden leg out of the coach. Now he slumped down as if he wanted to hide behind the others.

The worthy gentleman, unconcerned, kept on running. His forehead was covered with sweat. He paid no attention to the sneering shouts. He simply stared steadily through the lattice fence at the rolling wheels.

"He must be a madman!" cried one of the riders.

This was too much for Frutschnigg. He suddenly pulled himself together. "That," he said, "is a professor!" and it sounded sharper than he had intended.

"If that's a professor," bawled the man with the copper-red nose, "I'm the Emperor of China." He would have had the laughers on his side with even cheaper jokes.

But Frutschnigg was not to be intimidated. "The gentleman *is* a professor—Professor Simon Stampfer of the Technical College of Vienna! And I ought to know, for I am his laboratory assistant."

He quietly decided to pump the Professor, at the next opportunity, about his strange goings-on.

He had not changed his mind when, the next day, he carried the afternoon coffee into Professor Stampfer's workroom. Since the French, on May 21, 1809, at Aspern, had shot off his left leg and he had had to make do with the wooden leg, he had lost much of his agility; and now the fragrantly steaming drink, agitated by his unsteady gait, slopped over the edge of the cup.

He carefully put the cup to rights and laid beside it, with relish, the big croissant. This was really the right time to speak of what he had seen the day before on the road to the Vienna Woods. But Stampfer still sat in front of two heavy tripods that supported two cogwheels, cranked eagerly, and looked through the passing gaps of the nearer wheel at the more slowly turning farther wheel.

Frutschnigg hesitated. His memory of the silly tavern-seekers of the day before seemed to clash with the austerity of this room. To gain time, he hobbled to the window and looked out. He loved this view as much as Professor Stampfer did: over the bed of the Vienna River to the Bastion, with its old town gate, through which the traffic of this cramped capital and royal residence struggled, and above it all the lofty tower of St. Stephen's Cathedral. Knowing how much Stampfer loved the scene, a student of his had done a lightly colored drawing of it. The drawing now hung in the arch of the window, and Frutschnigg, because he was uncertain what to say next, stepped up to it to study it closely.

Stampfer's voice broke into his study: "The good fellow tried hard, but his carriages full of officers, his ladies in bell-shaped skirts with their foppish cavaliers, his saleswomen at their stalls under the Bastion—they all seem dead beside the picture that you can see through the window. The drawing lacks the most precious thing of all: life, movement! Isn't that right, Frutschnigg?"

It would certainly have been tactful for Frutschnigg to make some agreeable comment about either the drawing or the view. But, still thinking about his experience of the day before, he burst out: "The Professor is always thinking about movement."

"What do you mean by that?"

Frutschnigg came from the same village as Stampfer and therefore felt entitled to a certain freedom of manner. "Yesterday I saw the Professor running along a fence. The Professor was sweating, and I mean really sweating!"

Stampfer laughed. "Oho, so that's it!"

"If it please, Professor, I was riding by in a coach."

"And now you want to tell me that the people thought I was crazy."

"Not exactly that!" exclaimed Frutschnigg with pretended indignation. "But they *were* wondering a bit."

The Professor leaned heavily on the wooden crank, and his pale, narrow face was deeply serious. "Listen to me, Frutschnigg. People always wonder at first about those who look into a new, strange world. And I am one of those who look—or at least it often seems so to me. It began" —his glance wandered through the window and over the Bastion into the distance—"when I read about the 'bushy patterns' that some Englishman described somewhere or other. Those patterns really can be seen. All you need to do is to run along a picket fence and look through it at a rolling wheel. Then the wheel appears to be, not a turning wheel, but a hub with curved spokes growing out of it—a bushy pattern."

"That is not easy to imagine," Frutschnigg admitted honestly.

"But easy to see if you're not afraid to sweat. And it's not very hard to explain. The wheel is hidden by one fence picket after another. We see it only through the spaces between the pickets—in apparently isolated positions. And our eyes arrange these in a row, forming the bushy patterns."

"And the Professor sees all that when he runs that way?" Frutschnigg wavered between admiration and unbelief.

"That and much more! Once upon a time, when I first started to do my running, I noticed many other remarkable things—all examples of the 'stroboscopic effect'."

Frutschnigg looked bewildered.

"The stroboscopic effect!" Stampfer went on. "That probably means nothing to you—to you and to many others. But once it seemed to me to be the key to a door that would lead into an unexplored territory, into a new world."

The doorbell jangled. Even Frutschnigg felt that it rudely dispelled a strange and delicate mood.

He limped out to see who the intruder was.

"A gentleman, a major, would like to speak to you, Professor—a Baron von Hauslaab."

"Oh, that fellow!" growled Stampfer, and then he glanced anxiously over his shoulder to see whether Frutschnigg had dutifully closed the door behind him. This Hauslaab was, after all, a man one mustn't offend. He taught the sons of Archduke Franz Karl; indeed, he had complete charge of their education. He stood high at the Imperial Court and everywhere was highly esteemed because of his broad knowledge. Only a few people, to be sure, knew how he had acquired all this knowledge, but Stampfer had seen through him long before. Hauslaab dropped in occasionally—as if without particular purpose—and wormed the latest scientific findings out of him. He no doubt pumped other scientists in the same way.

"Nevertheless . . ." Stampfer shrugged. "There's no way out, Frutschnigg; you'll have to let him in."

Hauslaab rushed directly to the massive tripods, turned the crank unabashed, saw the front cogwheel turn and the back cogwheel turn. Then, looking at the Professor with narrowed eyes, he asked: "And what might be the purpose of this piece of machinery?"

Stampfer heard the mockery in his words—the mockery that the officer always let him hear, the mockery with which he irritated him into confiding his greatest secrets. This time too he fell into Hauslaab's trap, perhaps even deeper than before. He told about the bushy patterns. "And then Faraday, in the lead mills of Maltby, saw something interesting in two cogwheels mounted one behind the other on a shaft. Here you see that arrangement imitated."

"I am amazed," interrupted Hauslaab, sniffing, "that a man like Faraday, a man of international standing, concerns himself with such things."

Stampfer, absorbed in his problem, failed to hear the remark. "The two cogwheels are just right for showing this stroboscopic effect." He reached for the crank and put his face against the first wheel. "You see, if I look through a space of the front wheel at a cog of the rear wheel, the image of the cog formed on my retina lasts, as other experiments have shown, about a tenth of a second." He turned the crank. "Therefore this image is still there when the cog I looked at has been covered by the next cog of the front wheel. If now, when the next space arrives at my eye, the rear wheel has moved just fast enough so that another cog is in the position of the one I first saw, then the rear wheel seems to be standing still. See for yourself—there, the way it is now—look!" He cranked, looked, cranked harder. "What did you see?"

"Only your rather broad back," said Hauslaab mockingly.

"Excuse me," murmured the Professor, jumping away.

Now the officer looked through the gaps. "Very nice," he said, "very pretty, quite droll."

"If the next cog doesn't quite reach that position, so that when we see it through the next gap it is a little behind, we imagine that the cog, and the whole rear wheel, are going backward. We are convinced that we see a backward turning—as now . . ."

"It's a fact," confirmed the officer.

"But all the time I am still turning the rear wheel forward—only somewhat slower."

"Droll, really very droll," repeated Hauslaab.

"Only when our glimpse through the next gap seems to catch a cog farther along in the forward direction do we think we see a forward movement. This may actually happen when the rear wheel is running backward. I shall show you that too. Look, please . . . now!"

"Strange! And how do you account for that, Professor?"

Stampfer was eager to explain. "This stroboscopic effect is based on two processes, a physiological one and a psychological one. The physiological, bodily process is the persistence of an image on the retina after the stimulus has ceased. It is accompanied by a psychological, a mental process. If an object appears in a short enough time in two different positions that are not too widely separated, the human brain links the two images, and the object seems to move. If the object appears in a number of such successive positions, the impression of movement is strengthened. In our example we see the charming play of cogs . . ."

Stampfer worked with the frenzy of a man completely possessed by an idea. He heard nothing; he saw nothing, not even the bored expression of Hauslaab, whose curiosity had long since been satisfied.

Hauslaab's icy voice finally reached him like a reminder from another world. "Do you really believe, Professor, that this phenomenon has any significance?" It sounded exactly as provocative as it was meant to be. "Are you serious in assuming that it bears the germ of some advance—at least for technology?"

Stampfer slowly raised his head and looked into two cool, unsympathetic gray eyes. The rage rising in him made everything around him look red. How should he answer this conceited aristocrat? How? His head seemed about to burst.

Suddenly he saw that there was no answer. Grinding his teeth, he stood, as if turned to stone, silently facing the officer.

"You owe me an answer . . ." Hauslaab cleared his throat. Perhaps even to him what he was about to say seemed too bold. "So I make a proposal. You will surely not object if some day I bring along my friend Baron von Ettingshausen. Perhaps a talk with an expert will show you the next step. Perhaps he will know how to do something with this thingumajig."

Against such presumption Stampfer, the modest countryman, was helpless. He merely nodded as the officer, departing, casually raised his right hand to his cap. Then he sank heavily onto his chair. The narrow head with the long, flowing hair struck the cast-iron tripod, leaned against it, gratefully felt the cold metal. Stampfer was limp, tired, unutterably tired.

Tired? Wasn't it more than that? Wasn't it something completely different? And again his thoughts went round in the same track: "Quite droll! Do you really believe that this phenomenon has any significance?" That was the question! Was it not, indeed, the very question that had been stealing into his own mind, recently, whenever he looked through the fleeting gaps of the front wheel? What was he really trying to accomplish with his stroboscopic experiments? To what would they lead? To what result? To what use? Had Faraday asked himself this question? If so, he had said nothing. Did he say nothing because he had given the problem up, because it seemed too trivial to him? Or . . . or because he did not realize the phenomenon's significance, did not recognize the opportunity for progress that it offered? And just what was progress? . . .

It was already getting dark the next time Frutschnigg limped through the room. He noticed the untouched coffee and shook his head reproachfully. As a man from Stampfer's own village he felt entitled to play the motherly role: "You forget your bodily well-being, Professor."

Stampfer did not answer. His head still rested against the tripod, his mouth set in bitter lines.

The assistant felt that he could not simply go out and close the door behind him. He moved heavily and emphatically to the window with the unmistakable intention of tearing the Professor out of his gloomy brooding. "And now the streets are going to be lighted by gas," he remarked. "The lamps are to be hung from brackets attached to the houses or to special posts. And there will have to be a pipe, laid in the house wall or in the ground, to carry the gas to each flame! All that costs money, a frightful amount of money, but it's real progress!"

Stampfer turned his head. "Progress?"

"Yes, real progress!" In his joy at having finally distracted the Professor, Frutschnigg went on eagerly. "In my opinion, you see, you can call something real progress only if everybody feels the benefit of it, even the little man. Just think, in this case, about Laboratory Assistant Frutschnigg—only as an example, of course! In the future, when he, with his wooden leg, steers his way home in the evening through the crooked streets, he will no longer stumble over every stone, step into every pot-hole, and skid on every blob of mud. If that isn't progress, I don't know what is! And look: I'm not the only one who will like it; everyone will like it!"

"That may be," said Stampfer, trying to stop Frutschnigg's unusual flood of talk. "Today, however, you will still have to suffer in the darkness; and be sure to let me know when you go so that I can bolt the door after you."

That was clear enough. The assistant understood and shrugged, resigned. All he said was: "Don't forget the coffee, Professor."

But Stampfer did forget the coffee. He also forgot to bolt the door. His thoughts, after much brooding, suddenly linked themselves into a chain, the first link of which—how often it had happened!—seemed to hang from the hook called Chance: Frutschnigg was now hobbling painfully homeward . . . through the dark streets . . . gas lighting would make it easier for him . . . that would be progress, he thought . . . what was it the old babbler had said? . . . you can call something real progress only if everybody feels the benefit of it . . . wasn't that a hint? . . . a hint for him, for Simon Stampfer and his problem? . . . what good would it do anybody to see wagon wheels as bushy patterns or to watch a turning cogwheel? . . . he must provide, in place of the cogs, something familiar, something appealing . . . and it must have what he missed in the drawing beside the window, what made the view of the city so fascinating that it was hard to tear himself away from it: movement, life! . . . a rolling carriage would entertain people more than a circling cog.

Stampfer felt the pressure of his new idea. He would have to replace the cogs by pictures, each of which would be only slightly different from the next. He would have to paste the pictures to a cardboard disk, which would take the place of his rear cogwheel. A disk with slits cut in it would take the place of his front cogwheel. The two disks would turn at the same speed. But it wouldn't make any difference, really, if he used only one disk, one with slits, and pasted the pictures to the back of it. He would then have to set the disk up in front of a mirror. Maybe the second way would be simpler. The important thing was that one should see picture after picture through the passing slits and that the "cogs"—the parts of the disk between the slits—should cover and conceal the change of pictures. That would be a wheel that could show things moving, show movement—and life. A "wheel of life"!

Suddenly he hesitated. He thought of the wide, richly organized panorama outside his window and compared it with the narrow spaces between the cogs of the wheel. No, that wouldn't work! Not even a master could compress such abundance into such little pictures—which, besides, could differ from one another only slightly.

But must he start right off with such a broad, various picture as his favorite view? Wouldn't a detail, a simple little movement, be enough, at least for a beginning—something like a running dog, a jumping boy?

When, next morning, Frutschnigg arrived to assist the Professor at the class in applied geometry, he was surprised to find the door unbolted. He sneaked as quietly as he could into Stampfer's inner room. He saw that the magnificent croissant, which had cost a whole kreuzer, lay untouched beside the empty cup. The Professor had gone to sleep over eight pictures, all of the same size, which showed a ball-throwing Chinese in eight different positions. He was sleeping so soundly that even the noisy activity of his assistant did not disturb him.

For three days Stampfer would not see anybody. Then he called in Frutschnigg, in a loud and urgent voice, at an unusual hour, and was obviously in high spirits. The assistant had to sit down in front of the tripod. In the place of the familiar cogwheel he saw a cardboard disk with slits. To its back—the side not facing him—were pasted the eight pictures of the ball-throwing Chinese, and these were reflected in a mirror set up behind the disk.

"I shall now demonstrate for you my Stroboscope," said the Professor seriously, and he began to crank the disk.

After he had shown his assistant three times how he must hold his head, Stampfer won his first success. Frutschnigg grinned. "Why, it looks as if the Chinese were throwing the ball, catching it, throwing, catching—over and over."

"Do you like it?"

"Of course I do. It's fun to watch it."

"Understand, now, Frutschnigg!" Stampfer spoke solemnly, as if he had to justify himself not only to his assistant but to all humanity. "It's really only a slight difference, in principle, when the Chinese appears in the mirror instead of the cogs. It's only one step forward, a small step, but perhaps just the one that's needed for real progress—for the kind of progress that everyone can enjoy." Would this idea sound familiar to his assistant? "That's why I ask you, Frutschnigg: Do you believe that living pictures of this kind would interest other people too?"

Frutschnigg, thus asked for his opinion, relaxed and grew loquacious. "Why, of course they would! People are so curious, you know; they like to look at things. You should go out more, Professor, and find out what people look at when they have a little free time. They crowd into the shabbiest halls, there in the Prater, to see magic-lantern pictures. Phantasmagorias they call them—things that make your hair stand on end. Twenty kreuzers the show costs, although it hardly lasts twenty minutes." Stampfer's attentive silence increased his assistant's familiarity. "And I understand why they go there, Professor, I really do. What should people do with their leisure? They are grateful for every change. They like to look at something new even if it's the greatest nonsense."

"That's enough for me," growled Stampfer.

When Stampfer looked back over the years of his tentative experiments, his doubts, and his compulsive zeal, the results seemed to follow at a headlong pace. He obtained a two-year patent, dated May 7, 1833, on his Stroboscope. A well-known Viennese publisher agreed to print the disks on his presses: pictures of a dancing couple, a jumping boy, a woman at the well, and a number of other subjects, besides the ball-throwing Chinese. These were sold with a wooden handle on which they could easily be mounted and turned by hand. "The extraordinary enthusiasm with which our new optical illusions were received," announced the publisher in July, "has made it necessary to bring out a new and improved edition, on eight double disks." Simon Stampfer, at forty, had achieved a considerable success.

One day, not long afterward, Hauslaab strutted into Stampfer's study, followed by his expert, the highly dignified Privy Councilor Andreas von Ettingshausen, and bringing with him a cloud of cool reserve. "Perhaps you will show my friend Ettingshausen your thingumajig, there, your . . . uh . . . your Stroboscope."

The Professor of Physics at the University of Vienna, omitting any friendly gesture, made himself comfortable on the chair in front of the apparatus.

Stampfer, with the love and pride that every father feels toward his child, began to lecture. He explained the stroboscopic effect and then demonstrated the operation of his apparatus. "Two things are worthy of attention here, Herr Colleague," he concluded, speaking, in his eagerness, with more vehemence than the situation demanded. "First, for about half of the time you see nothing except the disk that alternately conceals and reveals the pictures; second, the illusion of activity is produced by pictures that are, within themselves, at rest."

Ettingshausen, ignoring the "Herr Colleague" (Stampfer, after all, was only at the Technical College, not at the University), leaned back comfortably. "For pictures at rest," he said, "they are somewhat too restless."

"That's the fault of the continuous movement," the sedulous Stampfer assured him, ignoring the jest. "The movement should really be intermittent: the pictures should move by jerks while they are covered. That is the next task, the next step in our progress. It's the same in all problems: the general desire urges us on, shows what the needs are. And I should rejoice at any suggestion serving that purpose—just as I rejoiced at Horner's Magic Drum, as laymen call it. I recognize it, without envy, as a handier and therefore more successful form of my Stroboscope. You must know it—a circular drum, turning on a vertical axis, with a series of slits in its upper half. Through the slits one watches a strip bearing successive pictures, which is inserted, inside, in the lower half. By this method the moving picture seems quieter. If a similar happy idea for moving the pictures should occur to you, Herr Colleague . . ."

Ettingshausen ignored this challenge and turned to Hauslaab. "This seems to be, in essence, merely an application of the principle that my colleague Plateau, at the University of Ghent, has been investigating and has recently made public. People call his apparatus a Phenakistoscope."

Then Stampfer lost his temper. "I swear to you," he said, "that this is the first time I've heard of this Phenakistoscope. And, besides, it's not important, in the long run, whether the idea was conceived by me or by somebody else. The important thing is that the time is ripe for fulfilling a general desire, that this apparatus can be improved, completed, developed into a world-shaking invention in which all mankind would be interested . . ."

"Let us not depart from the facts," interrupted Ettingshausen coolly, his eyes narrowed; then he turned back to Hauslaab. "Plateau, by the way, is young but has already done some brilliant work. He injured his eyes several years ago by staring at the sun, but I still expect great things from him. It seems odd that such a man should have taken time out to invent this little plaything." Ettingshausen nodded toward Stampfer's Stroboscope. Hauslaab contributed a smirk.

No one spoke for a while. Then Hauslaab said: "I should find fault with this apparatus, in the first place, because it is accessible to merely one individual at a time—and to that one only with some difficulty. In addition to that, the various scenes seem to me to be all too brief: they must offer more. But perhaps one cannot demand more of a plaything."

Stampfer remained silent. He could not say a word.

After Frutschnigg had closed the outer door behind the two visitors, a terrific crash spun him round. As he hurried back through the inner doorway, the Professor, leaning on the windowsill, even his lips pale, his gaze fixed on the Bastion, said: "Remove the ruins of that world-shaking invention!"

The assistant looked where Stampfer's outstretched arm pointed: to a heap of broken glass, crumpled sheet metal, and splintered wood. Bewildered, he hesitated.

Then Simon Stampfer straightened up to his full height. "Did I say 'invention'? That was presumptuous of me, Frutschnigg. I meant to say: Remove the ruins of my world-shaking plaything!"

3.

WHAT IS ACCIDENT?

"I HAVE lined up example after example, Nicéphore,
each more striking, more convincing, than the last. And
they show that astrology is not, as you used to say, a weak
support for weak souls." Colonel Niepce ended with a gran-
diloquent gesture. "Astrology is a science! Right?"

"No," answered Nicéphore calmly. With great care he
was cutting pieces of paper.

The Colonel became sharp. "And why not, revered
Cousin, if I may ask?"

"Because I cannot imagine how my whole life, with all its
joys, sorrows, and complications, could be determined by the
fact that I was born on March 7, 1765, in Chalon-sur-Saône."

"It isn't determined by that fact, as I've just explained
to you again, but by the position of the stars, and especially
by *your* star."

Nicéphore Niepce put down his shears and paper in order
to take his head in both hands. "What a zigzag path the star
that determines my life must have! Just think what it has had
to put up with: I grow up in an ecclesiastical seminary; then
I'm a lieutenant in the victorious French army in Italy and

spend six years as administrator of the district of Nizza; then, after my return, I build a motor with Claude and get a patent on it from Napoleon; now, for some years, lithography has fascinated me, and I'm even supposed to be an expert at it, but will that last? And a star is supposed to keep up with me? There's no star foolish enough."

His long-legged cousin would not give up. "Your erratic life is just another proof, Nicéphore! Who is to blame for all your ups and downs if not the stars?"

"Circumstances, my dear fellow, the conditions of life! It was the glorious Revolution that enticed me out of the seminary—you know it as well as I do—and the victorious Bonaparte that enticed me to Italy. And it was a contagious disease that forced me to give up military service. And you know perfectly well that I became an engineer because my brother Claude is a mechanic. And if I then turned to lithography, that also has a perfectly natural explanation: a man you know—I won't mention any names—had just stolen the secret of lithography from Alois Senefelder and had brought it from Germany in Napoleon's defeated army."

The Colonel twiddled his thumbs.

Nicéphore looked over his imposing array of bottles, apparently without finding what he wanted. He called his son, Isidore, and asked him to look in the cabinet for the bottle of highly rectified alcohol while he himself tested the quality of the yellowish-gray guaiacum.

"To speak of something reasonable," he began after a while, "I do hope that you will look up Chevalier & Son when you get to Paris. They carry on the big optical business in the Palais Royal and produce a camera obscura with a special lens, invented by them. You will buy it, for it is the only thing that will help me in my new experiments. Understand?"

Colonel Niepce, bored, twisted the creases of his haggard face. "Of course I understand, Nicéphore, now that you have explained the business to me for the twelfth time."

"And you won't forget?"

"My dear cousin, I have never yet forgotten anything except what I wanted to forget."

"That's not very reassuring."

"Besides"—the Colonel leaned forward confidentially—"I shall plan my trip so that I arrive in Paris on January 12, for that day stands under an especially favorable star."

"Oh, forget that stuff!" growled Nicéphore.

Colonel Niepce arrived in Paris, as he had planned, early on January 12, 1826, and he went that very morning to see Vincent and Charles Chevalier. Charles waited on him graciously, extolling the quality of his products in general and of his camera in particular. After remarking that the gentleman's commission from his cousin revealed an expert, a man of experience, he asked about the purpose for which the cousin was thinking of using the excellent apparatus.

The Colonel began to praise Nicéphore's work in lithography, celebrated the persistence with which, for more than ten years, Nicéphore had carried on his own experiments, and described the extensive stock of chemicals in the Niepce house, mentioning substances whose names really meant nothing more to him than memories of bad smells. Then, suddenly, he remarked that his cousin, at the moment, was really not occupied with lithography at all, for the printing of drawings no longer satisfied him. Nicéphore wanted to take pictures directly from nature, and that was how he had hit on an entirely new idea: he wanted, by some chemical process, to preserve, to fix forever, the pictures that appear at the back of the camera obscura. He was always talking about what he called heliography—that is, writing, recording an image, with the light of the sun. Finally the Colonel showed Chevalier one of Nicéphore's heliographic pictures. It was of the wrought-iron fence beside Nicéphore's house in Gras, near Chalon, and its quality astonished the optician.

"Extraordinary!" cried Chevalier as he handed back the

metal plate. "My camera will be just right for that work."

"Unfortunately not all his plates are successful. Most of the experiments he is doing now do not satisfy him at all."

When Charles Chevalier nevertheless asked for more details, the Colonel cleared his throat in embarrassment. In the first place, he said, he was no expert; in the second place, his cousin talked about his experiments only with his son Isidore and his brother Claude.

The businessman understood at once. "I was not trying to get at your secrets, sir; I know how anxious inventors are. In all innocence I simply wanted to tell you that I have another customer, a painter named Daguerre, who has apparently set himself the same task and at the moment seems likewise to have reached a standstill. I simply thought that it would be advantageous for both gentlemen if we could bring them together. But it was only a passing thought." He pushed the thought to one side with an elegant wave of the hand.

But the Colonel suddenly remembered that that day, the twelfth of January, was controlled by an especially lucky star. On such a day one must exploit every opportunity that comes along. He therefore wrote Nicéphore's address on a slip of paper. The optician, after putting the slip in his desk, surprised the Colonel with a new idea. "Don't you want to get in touch with the man yourself, Colonel Niepce? Mr. Daguerre lives at 15 Rue de Marais. There he thrills the curious public with his Diorama, a charming invention; panoramas, covering a whole wall, of strange, distant cities, in varied lighting. There you have change, movement, exactly what the public greed for sensation demands—and has demanded since the time of the Caesars! If I am not deceived, he will be interested, for his own purposes, in—pardon me, what was it you called it?—oh, yes, heliography! He will want to use it to improve his exhibitions—although his Diorama, without exaggeration, is already known far beyond the borders of France. It is something that visitors from the provinces should certainly see. You would have a pleasant evening there."

The Colonel's curiosity had been so aroused that as dusk fell he entered the Rue de Marais. At No. 15, in the painter's studio that towered above the third floor of the narrow house, a group of idlers in their Sunday clothes had already assembled. A half hour's waiting increased the suspense. At last a squat man entered and faced the audience—a man in whom everything seemed to be round: his nose, his cheeks, his eyes, his whole head framed in wild curls.

"That is the Master himself." The gentleman in the next seat, dressed in festive black, leaned toward the Colonel. "Louis Jacques Mandé Daguerre."

The Master, standing before the screen, bowed politely and expressed his joy at being able to offer a unique pleasure to his highly esteemed audience. He paid tribute to his partner, with whom he had opened the Diorama four years before, and to the master under whom he had begun to study painting when he was sixteen. "What I learned from him about the art of painting you yourselves may judge." The Colonel had the impression that this man—with all modesty—understood perfectly how to set his work in the right light. He wondered, however, why such an able businessman should wear himself out with experiments as futile as those of Cousin Nicéphore.

The room was darkened.

On the screen appeared an alluring Italian landscape: cypresses stood in the foreground, ruins and colorful houses behind them, and over an intensely blue streak of sea Vesuvius towered in full activity. Even before the last expressions of rapture had died away, the scenery gradually changed before the eyes of the spectators: it became darker and darker, outlines became indistinct, and finally evening settled over the recently sunny landscape.

Colonel Niepce felt a light pressure on his arm, on his

chest, as the elegant gentleman sitting beside him addressed him again. "The screen, made of a fine, transparent stuff, is painted, of course, on both sides—with the same landscape— and is lighted first from the front and then from the back. It's Daguerre's patent—just a trick, but executed in a masterly way." The man had probably recognized him as a provincial, thought the Colonel, and he was not sure whether he should resent the scorn implied by such recognition or welcome the man's obvious kindness.

On the screen, in colorful succession, appeared chateaus of the Loire valley, Naples, and a port in Sicily, first in brilliant sunshine, then in evening twilight. Even human figures that were clearly seen at first disappeared quietly from the pictures as the illumination changed.

Just as quietly, the Colonel realized when the studio lights were turned up, his kindly neighbor had disappeared—and with him the Colonel's wallet.

The Colonel was indignant, at first, at the meanness of the man who would take advantage of Daguerre's invention in this way, but then he remembered that the day, in his unshakable opinion, stood under an especially lucky star, and he consoled himself with the thought that his wallet contained no more than twenty-five francs. Nevertheless, any desire he had had to negotiate with the Master had disappeared.

Not only Colonel Niepce but Charles Chevalier also later remembered the twelfth of January. Daguerre was leaving the optician's shop that afternoon when Charles cried, "Just a moment, Master!" When the painter rolled his round eyes toward Chevalier, the latter was rummaging in his desk. "I have here the address of a man who seems to be using the light of the sun, as you do, to produce natural pictures."

Daguerre's right hand reached peevishly for the point of his collar, which was about to disappear behind his broad black cravat. "I was really thinking of giving up that nonsense. I'm not making any progress, though I've sacrificed plenty of time and money. Either I am too clumsy, or we are all chasing a phantom, a mirage."

"Don't say that, Mr. Daguerre!" sounded the voice of the optician from under his desk. "This morning I had in my hand a picture made by this Mr. Niepce, and it was simply superb. You should come to an understanding with him. Co-operation! Four eyes see more than two! If you will have just a moment's patience, I shall give you the address." He again jerked open one drawer after another.

"Don't bother," said the painter. "I'm through with that nonsense—forever. The commissions I've received lately from the theaters are all I can handle—and they pay better."

"A letter doesn't bind you to anything. Ah, here it is!" The optician triumphantly waved the paper bearing Niepce's address. "I know, you see, that nothing ever gets really lost here. Well, now, don't you want to try? Write to him!"

Reluctantly Daguerre reached for the paper. "I can't write to a complete stranger out of the blue like that . . . especially about such a ticklish affair."

It turned out that he could write, after all—but not until the end of January, after two weeks of proud resistance to Chevalier's suggestion. Then his curiosity, and the interests he had cultivated for years, conquered his pride.

Nicéphore Niepce answered him, and thus began a scanty correspondence, which suffered from both writers' reserve. Both were afraid to give away too much of what they had learned. They first began to trust each other when Niepce, on a trip to London to see his brother Claude, sought out Daguerre on his way through Paris. The painter was impressed by the tall, slim man, whose head, with its narrow aquiline nose, reminded him of the busts of ancient Romans; and Niepce, on his side, liked Daguerre's Diorama.

Not until three years later, however, did they really begin to work together, and it was Nicéphore that took the decisive step. He had finished a great number of discouraging experiments with various preparations, which were darkened by sunlight only after exposures of ten or twelve hours; the shadows moved during that time, of course, producing flat, fuzzy pictures. Nicéphore, now sixty-four years old, despairing of being able to finish his life's work alone, and tired of the fruitless correspondence with Daguerre, suggested a notarized contract, and one was finally signed by the two men on December 14, 1829.

The first article read: "Under the name Niepce-Daguerre, Messieurs Nicéphore Niepce and Daguerre set up a partnership for joint work on the perfection of the said invention made by Mr. Niepce and improved by Mr. Daguerre."

Niepce turned over his invention: Well-polished metal sheets, plated with silver, were covered with a very thin, uniform layer of special bitumen—a mixture of pitch and spike oil. The reddish layer, after long exposure in the camera obscura, was developed in a mixture of white mineral oil and spike oil and then thoroughly rinsed with water. In order to darken the shadows and thus improve the contrast, Niepce recommended, quite incidentally, that the plate then be exposed to iodine vapor in a sealed container.

Daguerre, for his part, contributed the equipment for a darkroom, his talent, and his skill—not much at first. But two years later it was he that made the decisive observation. Apparently he had been doing some experiments in which he exposed silvered plates to iodine vapor before exposure in the camera.

He wrote to Niepce: ". . . I had left a spoon lying on an iodized silver plate. After a while I saw, to my astonishment, that the spoon, through the effect of light, was perfectly silhouetted on the plate. I concluded from this that, contrary to your opinion up to now, the iodine does not simply darken the shadows; instead, it is the sensitivity of silver iodide to light that produces the heliographic picture . . . "

Nicéphore Niepce handed the letter to his cousin, who,

despite the oppressive summer heat, had come with the post-chaise through Chalon to Gras. "This proves," he said, "that the layer of silver iodide is sensitive to light, and Daguerre deserves the credit for realizing its significance to heliography. This is a real advance in our work." Nicéphore was sincerely pleased.

Colonel Niepce glowed with satisfaction and personal importance. Convinced that he had contributed to this success, he reminded his cousin once more that this fruitful cooperation had really come about through him—or, perhaps it would be better to say, because of that propitious January day.

Nicéphore failed to agree; the old story bored him. But his long-legged cousin persisted. Who had spoken to Chevalier about Nicéphore's work? Who? And who had left Nicéphore's address with the optician—not because he was urged to, but of his own accord? And why had he done it? He simply asked: Why? There was only one explanation for all this: his destiny, decreed for him by the stars, was that he should bring the two—Niepce and Daguerre—together.

Nicéphore, who was suffering from the extraordinary heat, laughed aloud in spite of his troubles. "Today, when two persons who are occupied with the chemical effect of light meet each other, the meeting is neither an accident nor something that needs a supernatural explanation. I should think it a miracle if they did not meet."

That night, July 5, 1833, he died of a stroke.

Isidore, as his father's heir, took Nicéphore's place in the contract with Daguerre. Two years later the contract was amended to change the name of the partnership from Niepce-Daguerre to Daguerre-Niepce, the change reflecting Daguerre's greater importance in the work. The partners did not consider their process ready to be made public. They wanted to improve it still further.

To his darkroom Daguerre devoted every hour he could

spare from his Diorama, every franc he could scrape together. He had given up Niepce's use of bitumen. Untiringly he covered copper plates with thin layers of silver, which he converted, by means of iodine vapor, into silver iodide. He exposed these plates to the light in his camera for a long, long time—forever, it seemed—until the desired pictures appeared on them. Always he kept changing the chemicals, their concentration, the order in which they were used. A simple solution of table salt proved to be the most effective means of fixing the pictures against artificial light.

His results did not satisfy him, but years passed while he was achieving them. Then he took the second decisive step.

He had put away in a cabinet, before any images had become visible on them, some plates that he had not had time to expose long enough. He was annoyed because the necessity of long exposure was always spoiling his painstakingly prepared experiments; and, to get the plates out of his sight, he had stuck them away in the top drawer. When, weeks later, he took them out in order to use them again, he could hardly believe his eyes. The despised plates mocked him with pictures of startling quality. Nothing was easier than to jump to the conclusion that he owed this success to one of the various chemicals that were stored in the cabinet. But which one? Daguerre methodically removed one chemical after another and each time put into the cabinet a freshly prepared, underexposed plate. And each plate, after a few hours in the dark, mocked him with a completed picture. The cabinet was enchanted: it seemed to know more than busy human brains.

Daguerre finally discovered its secret. His astonishing success was due to a bowl of mercury, the last substance he would have suspected. He now remembered, however, that mercury vaporizes even at room temperature. So . . .

He showed Isidore a whole series of his new pictures. Isidore was amazed.

"I can explain what happened only in one way," said Daguerre. "The silver iodide, which decomposes in proportion to the strength of the light falling on it, leaves the most silver at the spots receiving the most light. Silver in such finely divided form is, as you know, very dark; but it combines with the mercury vapor to form the white silver amalgam. The unexposed, undecomposed silver iodide is washed out by the hot solution of salt, leaving the dark background bare."

Isidore saw the significance of the new process. "And you made these pictures with underexposed plates. That means that the mercury vapor not only improves the quality of the pictures but shortens the exposure!"

"Yes, a great deal! I estimate that I can get results with only a sixtieth of the previous time."

Young Niepce was enthusiastic. "This discovery is unique, Master! We need have no anxiety about making it public. But doesn't it seem ridiculous that we owe it to an accident?"

Daguerre became thoughtful at that. "What is accident? Do you really think it's an accident when, among the thousand variables of an experiment, one combination gives a usable result? Isn't it merely a question of the time when this 'accident' will happen? Couldn't we just as well call it an accident when nothing remarkable happens?"

Isidore had no answer to that.

On January 7, 1839, Professor François Arago, enthusiastic about the Daguerreotype, announced the new process to the French Academy of Sciences. He amazed all his hearers by the extravagance with which he emphasized the significance of the new art of heliography. "By its general usefulness it will serve the fine arts, and it will undoubtedly bring science benefits that we can hardly foresee. Here is one that I do foresee: The monuments of Thebes and Memphis bear millions of hieroglyphs. Troops of artists have taken decades to draw them. From now on such things can be copied with the greatest accuracy in only a few hours."

A few months later, Arago, exerting the full force of his great prestige, demanded that the state reward Daguerre by buying his process, for the interests of inventors, he said, could not be sufficiently protected by the ordinary patent laws. The Chamber of Deputies thereupon approved a life-long pension of 6,000 francs a year for Daguerre and one of 4,000 francs for Isidore Niepce.

On August 19, at the Academy of Sciences, Arago made public all the details of Daguerre's process. In the fourth row, near the stove, half concealed by Jean Baptiste Biot, sat Privy Councilor Ettingshausen, Professor of Physics at the University of Vienna.

Ettingshausen left the hall with Biot and Gay-Lussac. He was quiet and thoughtful. The same unfamiliar train of thought occupied all three professors, and Biot finally gave expression to it.

"I should like to recite for you, gentlemen, a long list of resounding names: first Johann Heinrich Schulze of Halle, undoubtedly the first to discover the sensitivity of the silver salts to light; then Beccaria, Scheele, Senebier, Rumford, Ritter, Davy, Seebeck, and Gay-Lussac here. Frenchmen and Germans, Englishmen and Italians. I could name dozens more, and I know that hundreds who never attracted public attention deserve to be mentioned. They all busied themselves with the chemical effects of light—to develop the theory of light or to serve the purposes of chemistry, pharmacy, or biology. Ask the man on the street—the best-educated one, for all I care—what he knows about all these men. Nothing, of course! And then along comes our friend from Cormeilles-en-Parisis, the son of a court usher, a painter, and he unites all the many established facts into a—well, what shall we call it? Anyway, the whole world seems to be going crazy over his so-called heliography! It is becoming a joke. Do you understand it, gentlemen?"

They continued on their way. Then Gay-Lussac spoke. "Perhaps it's because this heliography—or photography, as Herschel calls it—appeals to everybody, can be understood by everybody—because everybody can take part in it, can use it to make his life more enjoyable. Even if all that is not yet possible, everybody hopes that it will be in the future—and rightly so."

Biot stopped and drew himself up in the pale light of a gas lamp. "You will certainly not, in all seriousness, Monsieur Colleague, maintain that the value of an investigation, of an invention, depends on whether or not the average citizen has a share in it!"

Gay-Lussac did not reflect long before answering. "That's exactly what I do maintain! What is the value, after all, of a discovery or an invention that is of no use to anyone, makes no one happy, that simply waits, in the dark corner of a scholar's study, for the end of the world? Isn't it like a precious pearl that you keep your whole life long in a safe-deposit box without ever letting anyone see it? I ask you, what's the value of that pearl? What do you get out of it?"

"Not a bad analogy!" admitted Professor Ettingshausen.

Not long before this, the house at 15 Rue de Marais had burned down. Daguerre's Diorama and his first heliographic works were destroyed. With amazing indifference he moved to the Boulevard St. Martin. When Arago commented on his composure, the painter shrugged and said: "Why not take the fire as a symbol? Dioramas are dead; the future belongs to photography."

Daguerre, in fact, turned out to be a clever businessman. He had sold his photographic process to the state; but use of the process, he told himself, required apparatus. With Alphonse Giroux, a tradesman of Paris, he turned to the manufacture of the apparatus. Every one of their simple little boxes bore his signature and Giroux's seal, and every one produced a considerable profit. The profits piled up into a fortune, but the bustling Daguerre was not satisfied: he himself took photographs. An "original daguerreotype" taken by him cost a hundred francs; other photographers charged twenty francs.

The daguerreotype process conquered the world as hardly

any invention had done before it. Its practitioners shot up like mushrooms out of the ground. Graphic artists, worried about their livelihood, expressed their anger in caricatures. Gay-Lussac showed one of these, by a well-known lithographic artist, to his colleague Biot. A crowd of people, in the picture, were pushing and shoving—to photograph and to be photographed.

"Are they lunatics or just enthusiasts?" asked Biot.

"Whichever they are, they confirm my expectations."

"And Daguerre is making money out of all this frenzy. An apparatus with plates and the necessary chemicals costs more than four hundred francs—a small fortune, an amount that many people have to live on for several months."

Gay-Lussac patted his colleague soothingly on the shoulder. "I know enthusiasts," he said, "who would pay many times that amount in order to get an apparatus without waiting. Ettingshausen, our Viennese colleague, is one of them. I found out that he took instruction in the new art from Daguerre himself."

Biot, worthy member of the French Academy of Sciences, shook his head. "A professor fussing with photography! Do you understand it?"

Among the distinguished men that were fussing with photography was an American, Samuel F. B. Morse, portrait-painter, President of the National Academy of Design, and inventor. Morse, while in Europe trying to get patents on his new electric telegraph, had talked with Daguerre, whom he knew as a fellow-painter, and had let Daguerre take a picture of him. On September 3, 1839, only two weeks after the details of Daguerre's process had been made public, he sailed for America on the *British Queen*, which was said to be the fastest ship of the time. He arrived in New York on September 20, bringing with him information about Daguerre's invention and also a camera that he had had built according to Daguerre's specifications. Within two weeks the newspapers of the eastern cities were publishing accounts of the new art of photography. Morse took his first daguerreotype with his new camera in that same month of September 1839, and in 1840 he opened what was probably the first school of photography in America.

Daguerre was made an officer of the Legion of Honor, a very special distinction in France; and that was only one of many honors. He received from Ferdinand, Emperor of Austria, a heavy gold medal and a box set with diamonds; and that was only one of many valuable gifts. He became rich and influential. He acquired a magnificent country estate. There visitors from all countries of the world besieged him, considered themselves lucky if they could shake his hand, luckier if they could be photographed by him, even luckier if they could photograph him, for Daguerre, the father of photography, did not like to be photographed.

Monuments were erected to him.

By 1850, Broadway, in New York City, was lined with "Daguerrean galleries" and "Daguerrean parlors," as the portrait studios were often called. The *Daguerrean Journal,* no doubt the first periodical devoted to photography, began publication on November 1, 1850, in New York. Even in America, Daguerre's name had become a concept.

On May 1, 1851, the first world's fair, an international industrial exhibition, was opened at the Crystal Palace, in London, by Queen Victoria of England. Photography was included among the arts and sciences, and photographers of six countries exhibited some seven hundred pictures, most of them daguerreotypes.

About the same time, however, an English sculptor named Archer announced a new photographic process, the wet-collodion process. When Daguerre died in July of that year, he could not have realized that the daguerreotype would soon be only a historical curiosity.

4.

BIG WINDOWS LET IN MORE LIGHT

"WHETHER we call it galvanism or electricity makes no difference. Whatever we call it, this new field of research will yield the energy of the future." The speaker leaned back in his chair. "Yes, of the future!" Unmistakable triumph radiated from his full beard.

Colonel Hauslaab seemed not to notice the triumph. He stood up, for he considered his scientific raid—his name for his unannounced visits to professorial chairs—at an end.

He had only wanted to replenish his knowledge enough to maintain his flattering reputation for omniscience, and he had allowed it to become late. Of what use to him was the extravagance of this learned man?

"I shall not fail," he said, and light mockery crimped his thin lips, "to pass on to the archducal sons entrusted to my erudition, during their study of the new knowledge, your quite youthful enthusiasm."

He took leave quickly, emphasizing the military manner. Then the tall door closed behind him, and he found himself standing in the dimly lighted corridor of the old university building. Darkness enclosed him. He cursed the stinginess of the building administration, which was still getting along with smoking oil lamps and was apparently opposed to the introduction of gas lighting, although gas had proved to be satisfactory everywhere, even for street lighting!

He felt his way cautiously. Involuntarily he stepped suddenly to one side to avoid a shadowy figure. His saber clattered against a column, and the medals on his chest jingled noticeably.

"Pardon!" apologized the shadowy figure.

"Oh, Ettingshausen!" cried the Colonel. He was obviously pleased to meet an old acquaintance. "Back from Paris, dear friend? From Paris! How I have been envying you! Do you share my feeling that one can think of Paris only in ecstatic expressions—wonderful, enchanting, charming . . . ?"

"With due respect for your enthusiasm, Colonel, I must say that to me Paris was, rather, just interesting. I was invited, remember, to a meeting of the Academy of Sciences. A Frenchman has developed a process that seemed important enough for France herself to acquire it. Arago talked about it, clearly, exhaustively, and—as he always does—charmingly, with the result that photography is trumps!"

"Photography! Well, well . . ." Hauslaab was immediately on watch again.

"I got in touch with this Mr. Daguerre—a simple man, by the way, a painter—and had him initiate me in the new art, which many extol as a gift from on high."

"And what do you think of it?"

"It's pleasant enough," answered the Professor, "but for my taste there is too much chemistry involved in it. I can't get used to the innumerable mixtures. So I have confined myself to spreading my knowledge here in Vienna, wherever there is an opportunity. A man named Martin, librarian at the Technical College, gets very pretty results. The process gives him much pleasure."

In the light of the flickering oil lamp the Colonel thought he read doubt in Ettingshausen's features. "But you don't think there's much opportunity for such pleasures in the future."

The Professor hesitated. "Well, I am skeptical. I am as reserved now as I was enthusiastic at first. It's the time, Colonel, the length of exposure that a picture requires. One must figure in half-hours, and even one half-hour lasts a long time! Not only is it hard to find subjects that will remain quiet so long, but the sun moves noticeably in that time, and therefore the shadows shift, the outlines change and become fuzzy. That is why the unadmitted goal of photography—the human likeness, the portrait—must remain an unfulfilled dream. Could you sit absolutely still for half an hour?"

"To remain quiet so long, Professor, would be more than a strain; it is, I should say, a pure impossibility."

"So you see!"

"But I also say that one ought to do something to change that condition. There must be some way to bring the time down to a humanly tolerable length."

Ettingshausen smiled grimly. "That sort of thing is always easy to say. But who do you think is capable of carrying out your idea?"

"You, for one! Can't you, with your optics, master this problem? Try lenses with great diameters. Big windows let more light into a room than little ones."

Ettingshausen nodded his head reflectively. "Not a bad idea, Colonel!" Hauslaab had awakened the ambition of the investigator. "These big lenses must, of course, have a short focal length, so that the screen—in this case the plate—can be brought close to the opening. The closer you get to those windows of yours, the brighter the light you get through them."

The Colonel laid his hand familiarly on the Professor's arm. "I know that the intensity of the light is inversely proportional to the square of the distance. Double the distance, and you get only a fourth of the intensity. Have I said that well?"

"Very well, Hauslaab, very well!" Ettingshausen's index finger pointed at the other's medal-covered chest. At this moment he was only the teacher; he would have acted the same at an examination. "And what conclusion do we draw from that, Hauslaab? If, with the same diameter, we could reduce the focal length to half of what it was, the light would be four times as intense. We must, therefore, demand the biggest possible lenses with short focal lengths. But such lenses must be calculated, Colonel, so that they will give a sharp image at every point of the relatively big plate. Such calculation requires mathematics, higher mathematics—the highest, I might say."

"Well?" said the officer. His gesture expressed an obvious challenge.

Ettingshausen turned up his nose. "It's true, as you may remember, that I love mathematics. But experimental physics fascinates me even more." He reflected a moment. "Anyhow, I may, if the occasion arises, talk to my young colleague Petzval. He's one to get excited about such a problem. Or"— a sly goblin seemed to whisper the idea to him—"why don't you try to solve it yourself?"

"Thank you, but no!" said Colonel Hauslaab, parrying. "Besides, I may soon be transferred to a course for Turkish officers. That may free me of the responsibility for my archducal sons, and I am glad of that after what I have just heard, for, what with all this enthusiasm for the new black-white art, my curious charges may wish to practice photography, and finally I might even have to take up alchemy."

Ettingshausen did find an occasion to speak to his colleague Petzval about the lenses or combination of lenses that photography, in his opinion, needed. The occasion was a granting of degrees.

Among the new doctors of philosophy, one with a chubby, youthful face attracted Petzval's attention. He nudged Ettingshausen and said: "That man radiates so much bliss and self-satisfaction into the world that one could envy him."

Ettingshausen knew all about him. "That is the former Student Luser, a prodigious idler who was going from bad to worse. You would be dumbfounded if you knew how many semesters he has behind him. Then photography was discovered; without that he might not be so far along as he is."

"Yes," joked Petzval, "the layman has no idea what possibilities the new art offers."

"You may laugh, but this Luser completed in a very short time, and submitted, a dissertation on the sensitivity of silver bromide to light, with special reference to heliography. His work not only opens new paths but shows that he has succumbed, body and soul, to photography."

Josef Petzval, Professor of Higher Mathematics at the University of Vienna, amazed and incredulous, raised his bushy eyebrows high. "Does all that really have anything to do with science?"

At that moment Ettingshausen remembered his conversation with Colonel Hauslaab. He began to talk about windows and intensities of light, about focal lengths and diameters of lenses. His argument occupied his mind so fully that he failed to notice when the others left the room. Petzval also failed to notice; the problem had gripped him.

"If you succeed, Colleague Petzval, in increasing . . . fourfold, let us say, the light-passing power of lenses, the exposure time will be reduced to a few minutes; then we may even think about photographic portraits, and then photography has a future—a future that we, perhaps, cannot even estimate."

That evening the lamp in Petzval's study burned for a long, long time. The new problem had taken possession of him because it demanded the limit of his mathematical powers. His lamp was to burn for many more nights.

Petzval began by choosing, as a measure of the light-passing power of a lens, the ratio of the lens's diameter to its focal length. He found that the ratio for Chevalier's well-known lens, which was built into Daguerre's camera, was 1/14. The focal length of the lens was fourteen times as great as the diameter of the lens.

This ratio he wanted to change, he must change! And not by a mere trifle but, if possible, to 1/10 or 1/8—or, still better, he would try right off to reach the ratio 1/6! The distance between the photographic plate and the lens should be only six times the diameter of the lens. How much light that would throw on the light-sensitive surface! How much shorter the exposure!

Petzval figured and figured. He took into account the density and the refractive index of the different kinds of glass and of air; the gathering power and dispersing power of lenses of varying curvature; the effect of cement between the lenses. He filled sheet after sheet with equations, logarithms, integrals. He was nearly overwhelmed by the apparently infinite number of derivations, by a real mathematical flood. In the meantime he discovered new laws of dioptrics, the science of refraction.

One day Ettingshausen strutted into his study, driven by curiosity, interest, and the feeling that he was involved in this problem. "Well, what are photography's prospects, Colleague Petzval? Have you yet reached the point where ten minutes are enough for an exposure? I have done some experimenting, and that is the very longest time that I could hold out in order to preserve my likeness for posterity."

Petzval did not take up the jovial tone. Thoughtfully he passed his hand over the ruff-like beard that stretched round his jaw from one ear to the other. "Colleague Ettingshausen," he finally said, "combinations of lenses are moody and refractory creatures. Sometimes they give a picture that's not good at all, sometimes one that's unavoidably distorted."

"Thanks, thanks!" said Ettingshausen. "I foresaw that the business would not be simple, but you'll manage it, all right."

He came again and again. He smiled, now relaxed and patronizing, now vague and indecisive. Petzval pointed to the constantly growing bundle of his calculations, but he avoided saying anything about them.

So the fall and winter passed.

It was already 1840 when Petzval reached the ratio 1/6.

Should he be satisfied with that? Now, when he had, in his field, attained a mastery that no one else in the whole world could equal? Ridiculous!

When the lilacs were blooming in the gardens and the sun was lighting his gloomy study with new force, Petzval stopped at the ratio 1/3.6. The focal length of his objective, his combination of lenses, was only about a fourth of that of Chevalier's famous lens. His objective would therefore let sixteen times as much light fall on the plate; compared with Chevalier's product, it was positively hungry for light.

The next day Petzval strolled into Ettingshausen's stiffly ceremonious study—casually, but with a joyous light shining from his eyes. "This objective," he said, holding up a drawing, "should cut the exposure time to a sixteenth of what it was, to one or two minutes—in bright weather even to thirty seconds. That will have to do—at least for the present."

"Do!" exclaimed Ettingshausen. "Do! Why, Colleague Petzval, this achievement makes our wildest dreams look timorous! It makes the cautious estimates of the experts look like the guesses of laymen! No one expected anything like this! With this objective you will need only a minute for a portrait. Do you know what that means? Photographic portraits are now possible!"

"That I knew all along," complained Petzval, "but the trouble is that I don't know anybody who can grind such a combination of lenses."

"Just a moment, Colleague Petzval!" Ettingshausen suddenly began to rummage through the stack of papers on his desk. "No, we must not miscarry on that job! Certainly not!" He dug into the desk drawer, first on the left side, then on the right, "There was a man here, you see . . . an optician . . . offered his services to me himself . . . for experiments. It was some years ago." He looked again at a bundle of papers, then drew out of it a slip that had already turned slightly yellow. "Here he is: Voigtländer—Johann Friedrich Voigtländer. It's a strange name; he can't be an Austrian. But he works in Vienna. Here you have his name and address."

Johann Friedrich Voigtländer cast a sidelong glance at the drawing in Petzval's hand. Then he leaned forward in order to see it better. Then he reached for it.

"Do you know what that is?" His voice was hoarse. "That's the job I've been waiting for—for years—for decades—my whole life long!" His calloused hand passed cautiously over the drawing, caressed it. "And now—it's too late!" Petzval noticed the weary tone as well as the strange gleam in the optician's eye. The man might be in his early sixties, Petzval thought, and apparently he no longer considered his eye accurate enough to execute such a work of art. Petzval feared for the outcome of his labors.

But suddenly the old man pulled himself together and stood up to his full height. There was, after all, his boy, Friedrich, now twenty-eight years old. He had gone through his father's strict school, which demanded the greatest accuracy. He would pass the test, for his future was at stake.

"We shall do it, all right, Herr Professor." Voigtländer said no more.

The young Friedrich Voigtländer had the objective ready in just a month, to Petzval's complete satisfaction. Father Voigtländer was proud and happy.

Petzval and the young Voigtländer built an experimental camera. It was made out of cardboard and shaped like the stump of a pyramid, with eight corners. The objective was in the smaller end of the stump, the plate-holder in the larger end.

Then the next problem appeared. Experiments on which a reliable judgment could be based demanded an expert in the craft of photography. Petzval applied to Ettingshausen and on his advice got in touch with Anton Martin, librarian. Martin was regarded as both the best and the most enthusiastic photographer in Vienna.

His daguerreotypes, made with Voigtländer's camera, were a sensation. The whole world demanded the new camera.

Friedrich Voigtländer worked from dawn until late at night. He needed now the driving energy inherited from his father, for this, he believed, was *his* objective, *his* camera—and *his* chance. But his strength alone was not enough. He was always looking for capable helpers who could wield the burin at the lathe and handle a file. He looked especially for competent lens-grinders. But he always did the final polishing himself.

Voigtländer's easily portable camera, made of wood or of brass, came onto the market. Supported by a stand with two Y-shaped forks at the top, it turned out circular pictures about three and a half inches in diameter. The outfit cost 120 guldens, about two months' salary of the average civil servant. Each was equipped with a Petzval portrait objective. Voigtländer made the camera by mass-production methods, but he could not produce enough objectives to satisfy the growing demand. An optician in France began to turn them out, and then two opticians in London. Voigtländer produced 1,500 objectives in the first ten years. He got for them a great deal of hard cash, which he carefully saved, for he was cherishing great secret plans.

And Petzval? He had only the honor of having calculated the objective.

In the next ten years Voigtländer produced 8,000 Petzval objectives and became a rich man. He invested most of his money in the factory he had built in Braunschweig in 1849.

And Petzval? He had, besides the honor, only the feeling

that he had been cheated. One day, when this feeling turned into a certainty, he fell out with Voigtländer, and the two parted as enemies.

Petzval sat down again at his desk, calculated again, devoted hours of every day and whole nights to an effort to show Voigtländer that he had still more to offer, could do still better. He created the Orthoscope, a powerful lens for pictures of landscapes. The optician with whom he allied himself was a master of his craft, but he was no Voigtländer. Poor business methods forced him to close his plant.

Petzval again came out empty-handed. Voigtländer, in the meantime, had greatly enlarged his factory in Braunschweig.

Once more Petzval retired into his quiet study. Again he began to calculate. Mathematical formulas without end filled sheet after sheet of paper and piled up to fill a thick file. Petzval delivered the data for an objective with the fantastic ratio $1/2$—an objective nearly four times as powerful as the one he had calculated for Voigtländer.

If Petzval had had a little more money, he might have been able to control the production of his new objective. But, lacking capital, he had to ally himself with a partnership of four opticians. The dream of success was short. Even all the men working together could not bring their camera on the market fast enough to get control of it or even to make Voigtländer feel their competition. The firm of Voigtländer continued to grow, thanks to the excellence of Petzval's first objective.

And Petzval?

When Privy Councilor Andreas von Ettingshausen reached the retirement age and gave up his chair at the University of Vienna, he paid farewell calls on his more intimate colleagues. Petzval was the last he called on, not only because he felt closest to him, but also because that was the hardest call to make now that he had seen the morning paper, which he had read earlier than usual because Dr. Luser—the man who considered himself the patron saint of photography—had called his attention to it.

The paper rustled in his breast pocket as he sat down opposite the mathematician. The ruff-like beard no longer fringed Petzval's jaw, but his mustache hung thicker and longer over his upper lip and mouth, and his bushy eyebrows grew rankly under a deeply furrowed forehead.

Ettingshausen suddenly felt the desire to say something consoling, something cheerful, to this disappointed man.

"As far as photography is concerned, Colleague Petzval," he began, "the picture has changed completely. Shortening the exposure time is still, of course, the first necessity. But right now we are offered one process after another for making the plates more and more sensitive to light. This chemical path seems to me the only one on which progress is still possible, for it was your unique service, Colleague Petzval, to follow the other, the optical path, to its very limit. At least that's the way an expert must see it. But . . ."

Petzval broke in without spirit. "Don't trouble yourself any further, Ettingshausen. I too have read the morning papers and have seen there that the Emperor has been pleased to raise Voigtländer to the nobility. And why? Because of his services to photography! Although I know how society today exaggerates the significance of that distinction, I learned of it without bitterness. How one takes something of that sort is largely a matter of temperament."

Ettingshausen sighed with relief. "I am very glad that you take it that way—more calmly than I did, I assure you. I felt the implied slight to your person as a gross injustice, for you deserved the major share of the credit for . . ."

"Ah, so you remember that I too had something to do with it!"

"Drop the bitterness, Colleague Petzval. You know that I not only say so here but everywhere else will always proclaim that the credit is yours. If I had my way, many things would look very different. If out of Voigtländer they can make a Lord of Voigtländer, out of you, the creator of dioptrics, they should have made a prince."

Petzval suddenly drew Ettingshausen close and spoke confidentially, smiling slyly, laughing his old roguish laugh. "That would not be possible!" he said; and, as his visitor looked at him questioningly, he went on: "I was born in Hungary, as you know, in 1807—on January 6, Three Kings' Day. There would be nothing remarkable about the date if my two brothers had not also been born on the same date— January 6, Three Kings' Day. This schedule of births in the House of Petzval is so obviously improbable that word of it spread and no one wanted to believe it. When, in 1835, I took up my post as lecturer at the university in Pest, it turned out that the unbelievable story had penetrated even to that place. I had to submit an official extract from the parish record and prove that I really had been born on Three Kings' Day. I wonder if the gentlemen were convinced. Only the inhabitants of our little town really believed it, knew it for a fact. They even made a joke of it and called us brothers the Three Holy Kings."

Now Petzval spoke close into Ettingshausen's ear. "Don't you believe that it would be a degradation if they made a simple prince or, worse, an ordinary lord of something or other out of a man who was born a king?"

5.

NO ORDINARY SERGEANT

THE cab, passing through·the old town gate, rolled over the swollen Vienna River toward the highway. Colonel Hauslaab tried to avoid the persistent rain by squeezing himself into a corner of the seat, but without much success. The raised top of the cab seemed a funnel to catch the drops.

The Colonel was in a bad humor—less, he was sure, because of the penetrating cold than because of the commission with which certain high authorities had recently honored him. Why had the high authorities had to choose him, of all people, to direct the course of instruction for the visiting Turkish officers—a course that was sure to be full of traps? For the fellows were certainly not coming to Vienna to learn to cry "Atten—tion!" or to shoot or even to ride. Now that so much ado was being made about the sciences, especially the technical ones, people imagined that they even had something to do with military affairs! One could be sure that that was the only reason why the Sultan, in the summer of the year 1840, was sending his officers to Vienna. And soon the troubles would begin. It would be easy, if necessary, to find someone for the "Atten—tion!" and the shooting, but who would teach mathematics, physics, and this new, remarkable science called chemistry? His last hope was Lieutenant Scheyer. If *he* didn't know what to do . . . !

He cautiously stuck his head out. They were just rumbling past a church that he recognized. He hoped that fool in the driver's seat had not forgotten that he must turn right to reach the artillery barracks.

The highly placed gentlemen must know very well what an awkward position they had put him into. If those Turkish skulls didn't learn to figure well and failed to understand the secret of steam power, the man responsible for their instruction would, of course, be considered incompetent. And in this case that man was unmistakably Colonel Franz Baron von Hauslaab. On the other hand, if everything went all right, what would he get out of the whole vexing business? A blinding decoration, accompanied by a letter of thanks from the Sultan! The All-Highest War Lord might at least make him a general!

The fool in the driver's seat had made the right turn, of course, and was glad himself when the cab left the bumpy road and glided over the faultlessly scoured courtyard of the barracks as if on a pastry board.

Hauslaab had himself conducted to Lieutenant Scheyer.

"Now don't stand on ceremony, Scheyer; sit down at ease with me," he ordered the surprised officer. "You must help me out of a terrible mess. I have, as you know, educated Archduke Franz Karl's sons. As a result, the authorities think I can do anything, even train a band of half-wild janissaries who are coming to Vienna this summer. As thanks for their teaching us to make coffee in 1683, we are to teach them physics and chemistry. You, of course, are the right man for the job, but you are indispensable here. The other officers serving under the imperial banners can only ride, play cards, and drink champagne. Where shall I get a suitable instructor, where? We cannot lay ourselves open to the Sultan's ridicule by appointing a civilian. A civilian!" He shuddered at the thought. "Through your work you know our men better. You are my last hope."

To his amazement the Lieutenant did not have to think for even a second. "I should like to recommend Artillery Sergeant Uchatius, Colonel."

"Uchatius? I never heard the name. And sergeant?" The Colonel made a wry mouth. "Don't be offended, Scheyer, but after all I can't assign an ordinary sergeant as instructor to Turkish officers."

"He is no ordinary sergeant, Colonel; he is my assistant."

"Phoo!" exclaimed the Colonel, and he looked with amusement into the Lieutenant's eyes. "Could you tell me something more than that about the man?"

Scheyer, the instructor in physics and chemistry with the artillery corps, stuck his chest out a few inches more. "Uchatius was transferred to the artillery corps almost ten years ago, in November 1830. I didn't really notice him, however, until four years later, when, after finishing his training, he was to be transferred again to the infantry. At that time he voluntarily took the position of laboratory assistant in chemistry, a service that was below his rank—driven by a desire for knowledge, as he later told me. In this subaltern position he acquired so much experience and knowledge in a single year that he was allowed to take the examination with the first-year students. After another year as laboratory assistant he passed the final examination. For three years he has been assistant instructor here, my right hand and our best man."

Scheyer had finished. The Colonel strummed with his fingers on the table top, and a mocking smile curled the corners of his mouth. "I see, Lieutenant Scheyer, that you know all about the man. Nevertheless, I should like to scrutinize him myself."

Dr. Luser let his legs dangle over the edge of the table. In the flickering candlelight that barely brightened the dark-room his face seemed even rounder and rosier than in daylight. He watched the sheet of straw-paper, prepared with silver nitrate and a solution of table salt, that Sergeant Uchatius was bathing in a basin. Uchatius had exposed it to the sun through a drawing made on glass and still hoped that the developer would bring out a picture on the sheet. He had heard that an Englishman was making photographs in this new way.

"Do you know, Uchatius, what surprises me the most about you?"

Uchatius continued to rock his basin.

"It's your extraordinary persistence. I too have an unusual enthusiasm for photography, but it doesn't equal yours. Repeating this attempt for the fiftieth time, you still have the energy to stare at that piece of paper in vain for two or three hours. Where did you get this tough will power?"

"From the Field of Stones," answered Uchatius quickly.

"From the Field of Stones? I never heard before that anything flourished there!"

Uchatius grinned. "I was born and brought up in Theresienfeld, Maria Theresia's colony for veterans, and I attended the school in Wiener Neustadt. Do you know what that means?"

In the dim light Dr. Luser's rosy, boyish face, as he shook his head, seemed still more naive.

"That means a walk of more than an hour—in sun and rain, in storm and snow, and crossing the Field of Stones. It also meant, for me, an unusual training of the will. I was a sickly child, and I had to cover that ground—running, dawdling, running—with a much stronger brother. And older, stronger brothers are hard, hard as rock."

Luser swung his legs awhile before he spoke. "And now you squander that magnificent energy on—it seems to me—a hopeless task."

"No!" exclaimed Uchatius. "Daguerreotypes cannot be the final answer, Doctor, even though your Mr. Kratochwila has improved the process by exposing the plates to chlorine vapor. Who wants to collect metal plates? I think paper has a better chance."

"Then at least try it with exposures made in a camera, not with these drawn copies. I see that I'm going to have to get one of his new miracle cameras out of my friend Voigtländer in order to put your stubbornness to good use."

Heavy army boots tramped by the darkroom door. The corporal on duty roared like an irritated bull: "Artillery Sergeant Uchatius, report to Lieutenant Scheyer at once!"

Without his cap, in a spattered, acid-eaten blouse, as always when his superior called him from his work, Uchatius rushed into the Lieutenant's room. It wasn't so much the service regulations that made him straighten up before his superior as the surprise at finding himself facing an arrogant and provokingly smiling colonel.

"So this is Artillery Sergeant Uchatius!" sniffed Baron von Hauslaab. "Not very imposing."

Scheyer was not easily disturbed. He answered matter-of-factly that volunteer gunner and officer candidate Uchatius, though he was only five feet one inch tall, had, "with indulgence toward his deficient length of body," been declared fit for service in the second regiment of field artillery.

"That too you know exactly, Lieutenant," sneered Hauslaab. His old distrust of commoners—who, in his opinion, always stuck together—made him seem more sarcastic than he wished to be. His fingers drummed his nervousness in the quiet room.

Finally, to relieve the tension, Scheyer added: "His father, too, was an instructor here. Mathematics and physics were among his subjects."

"Very well," answered the Colonel, indicating by a nod that his inspection of Sergeant Uchatius was finished.

"If the man does not suit you, Colonel," began Scheyer as soon as Uchatius had withdrawn, "I really don't know where to turn."

"You don't mean it!" exclaimed the Colonel, flaring up.

These commoners, it seemed to him, regarded knowledge and technique as their own exclusive domain. They pushed one another forward, and now things had got so far out of hand that they actually recommended any old sergeant as an instructor for officers!

And, as a matter of fact, he had no choice—having been saved, in a way—but to say yes and amen to everything.

At the same time he made up his mind to watch Sergeant Uchatius—constantly and thoroughly—from then on.

Anna was very proud of her Franz when, on Sunday, they wandered through one of the old town gates into the Prater. In his assignment as instructor she saw the cheerful beginning of a distinguished career—a beginning that he owed to his comprehensive knowledge. For that knowledge Anna had a mighty respect—more respect, Franz had once maintained, than for him.

But Franz Uchatius was not cheerful: he was remembering the Colonel's scornful face. "Not very imposing!" The provocative remark still rang in his ears, called forth contradiction, urged him to retort. But he was powerless. How could he oppose a man like Hauslaab? A dark cloud passed over his forehead and enveloped him in the oppressive melancholy that Anna knew well and feared.

"When this colonel sees what you can do," she said, "he will certainly make himself useful to you in other ways too. Perhaps, Franz, you will be transferred to a position from which you can get ahead better. Or, so that you will suit the officers better, he will make you a lieutenant—and then we can marry." That was, above all, her dream. But neither her cheerfulness nor the confidence that seemed to lie in the early spring air could drive away his depression.

Anna turned out to be right in a certain sense.

It was hardly a year later, and Uchatius happened to be working again in his darkroom. He liked to do this, and he did it as often as his duties and Anna Brandl permitted. He was working this time with special enthusiasm, for he had photographed Lieutenant Scheyer in the bright midday sun, and it was the first picture he had taken with the new Voigtländer camera that Dr. Luser had got for him. He had first treated the silver-coated copper plate with both bromine and chlorine as well as iodine, for Dr. Luser had convinced him that Franz Kratochwila's latest method increased the sensitivity of the plate at least fivefold; and, depending on Petzval's objective, he had exposed the plate for only thirty seconds.

He examined the progress of the development in the gleam of a shaded oil lamp. Scheyer's warlike mustache was already showing magnificently. He would, of course, fix the picture with sodium thiosulphate. Dr. Luser had advised him to use that compound, and so far it had worked wonderfully well.

But he didn't get to that point. A powerful hand rapped stormily at the barred door. "Artillery Sergeant Uchatius, come out at once!"

That sounded penetratingly military, and the technician Uchatius realized immediately that he was really only a tiny cog in the gigantic machinery of the Imperial Army. With a sigh he leaned his precious plate against the wall in the darkest corner. He hoped it wouldn't get spoiled.

His eyes not being adapted to daylight, he blinked as he walked into the bright outer room.

"Just as unimposing as he was before!" announced Hauslaab, who had, in the meantime, been made a general.

"Artillery Sergeant Uchatius has just been engaged in finishing a daguerreotype," explained Lieutenant Scheyer.

The General raised his eyebrows haughtily. "So you too spend your time on that fashionable frivolity!" And turning to Scheyer, he asked, "Is this activity suitable to a man who wears the Emperor's uniform?"

Again the Lieutenant defended his assistant: "Sergeant Uchatius is trying to find new methods."

"Oh, everybody's doing that today: Séguier in France, Goddard in England, the Natterer brothers here in Vienna, and Samuel Morse in America. Yes, even men who have to be taken seriously—such as Ettingshausen—are succumbing to this incomprehensible enchantment." By this speech he exhibited both his broad knowledge and his contempt for the not very warlike Uchatius, who responded only with increased embarrassment.

Again Scheyer intervened: "You will, by the way, strike your tents here, Sergeant Uchatius, for you are being assigned to the cannon foundry, I have just heard." He nodded hardly noticeably toward Hauslaab.

"And you owe that," added Hauslaab, "to your success in the training of the Turkish officers, not to these trivialities." The General pointed to the darkroom. "Nevertheless, so that you may see that I am no barbarian, you may show me your picture."

In the dull glow of the flickering oil lamp General Hauslaab looked at the successful portrait of Scheyer. For a moment Uchatius flattered himself with the thought that he saw recognition and pleasure in the General's features. But Hauslaab dispelled this impression at once with emphatic sharpness: "When I want a good portrait of myself, I'll turn to a painter like Danhauser or Kriehuber. One learns to appreciate such artists only when one sees a tin imitation like this. If you want to make an impression on *me*, Sergeant Uchatius, produce *moving* pictures."

Now, thought Scheyer, the General was making himself ridiculous.

The little Sergeant seemed even more helpless before this challenging mockery. "Moving pictures?" he asked vaguely.

"Yes, there is such a thing!" Hauslaab ground the words between his teeth. "Stampfer, at the Technical College—another comical fellow with a great taste for trifles—makes them—for what he calls his Stroboscope. He has even shown it to me. It's true that I didn't see very much, for in his enthusiasm he was usually blocking my view. The first thing to do with it is to make the performance more accessible—perhaps to a large group." He was now speaking only to the bewildered Scheyer. "And by the way, Lieutenant, have you ever realized what an advantage it would give us to be able to show a movement in all its stages—to exhibit, let us say, the trajectory of a shell? And I can even imagine that a moving picture of a human being would show many personal characteristics that are lost in a static picture, no matter how successful it is." He turned brusquely. "Yes! Make moving pictures, Uchatius!" It sounded like a military order.

At the door, surprisingly, he stopped a moment. He turned his head and sniffed over his shoulder, casually: "I really am amazed, Uchatius, that you had not yet heard of Stampfer's Stroboscope."

In the fall of 1841, when he was thirty years old, Sergeant Uchatius had begun his service in the cannon foundry. Since then he had been devoted to metallurgy, whether he was testing samples of molten metal or inspecting finished cannon, whether he oversaw the delivery of pig iron or supervised its processing. His whole life belonged to steel, to bronze, to other alloys—or, more exactly, his whole official life, for he still spent all his free time in the darkroom of the artillery barracks.

Lieutenant Scheyer was glad to have him continue his experiments in the darkroom, but not the vivacious Anna Brandl. She looked askance at his work, which General Hauslaab had called trivial, which her father, Artillery Captain Brandl, regarded as childish, and which stole her Franzl from her. He was so preoccupied, she was sure, merely because that stuck-up general had asked him for moving pictures. Franz did not realize it and certainly would not admit it, but she knew how he reacted to a challenge. Right after the General's unlucky visit to the barracks, Franz had got himself a Stroboscope, and not long after that a magic lantern

—both paid for with his own money when he should be saving every penny for their future home. And why? Merely to prove to Hauslaab and the world that even the impossible was possible for him if he tackled it with determination.

He had, indeed, bluntly told her his opinion: "Every problem is soluble if you only devote yourself to it intensely enough." And such devotion he obviously wanted to give to the improvement of Stampfer's living pictures.

When she did succeed in luring him out of his darkroom, what did he do? He described the difficulties of his task: he told her that the pictures should really be transparent, that he wanted to install a lamp in the middle of the Stroboscope but that all the lamps were worthless. One day he wanted to install an objective in front of every slit; the next day he had given up the idea because it would cost too much to carry it out. He rambled on about a thousand different things and plans—but not about the plans that engaged couples usually talk about.

After Franz had been serving in the foundry for a year, she insisted that they get married, hoping thereby to bind him closer. Nevertheless, he continued to spend his free time in the musty barracks darkroom, whose fumes were intolerable to a normal human being. All she accomplished was that he now came home to her on days when his failures especially discouraged him. On such days she had to call upon all her vivacity to bring him out of his depression.

Then, surprisingly, came that day when he grabbed her waist and whirled her round and round. "It's all really very simple," he explained. "All I need to do is to combine the Stroboscope and the magic lantern!" Anna believed that was the inspiration of a genius, but Franz made it all sound so matter-of-fact. He himself simply wondered about the strange nature of the human mind, which, when awake, could search for an answer in vain and then, in sleep, find the answer positively forced upon it, as if it had gone on working, independently, in its hidden depths.

On July 11, 1843, because of his outstanding achievements in metallurgy, Uchatius was made a lieutenant. Anna would have liked to go for a walk with him on one of the promenades of the city, but his experiments still left him no time.

One Sunday, however, he did take her out—not, to be sure, to dance in one of the vineyard gardens or to dine at Domayer's, the famous restaurant in the suburb of Hietzing, but into his darkroom at the barracks. There he brought out a black box, which had, in the front, a tube that reminded Anna of a cannon. Franz took it apart solemnly.

"In essence," he said, "it's a magic lantern. It has a lamp and, in front of that, a condensing lens that gathers the light and throws it through the objective"—he pointed to the tube—"onto the wall. With an ordinary magic lantern, the pictures have to be inserted, one after another; but here I have a disk with twelve transparent pictures rotating between the objective and the lamp, each picture a little different from the others—an idea that I took over from Stampfer. Here is the crank that you turn it with. Then, so that you won't see the pictures as they change (for then all you would see would be spots flitting by on the wall), I have, on the same shaft, an opaque disk with slits, which always cuts off the light while the picture is changing. So, Anna, you see a picture light up; while it persists on your retina, the light is cut off and the picture gives way to the next one, which is then projected on the wall through the next slit."

None of this was clear to Anna, but she gladly let herself be pushed into the waiting chair and stared at the dark wall.

"Now!" cried Franz. He began to crank furiously. On the wall appeared a dimly lighted circle, about six inches in diameter, in which a gymnast, with jerky movements, danced on a tightrope—again and again—tirelessly.

"What do you think of it, Anna?"

"Is that all there is?" She thought of the four years he had devoted to this pale, rickety, jerky dancer.

In his inventor's rapture he seemed not to hear her disappointment. "It took men thousands of years," he said, "to invent the wheel so that they could replace gliding friction with rolling friction, thousands of years to print a book with separate letters. And shouldn't it have been obvious all the time that they could cut single letters instead of whole pages?"

Anna saw that she had nearly committed a great stupidity, and she was thankful for his exultation, which bubbled over her tactlessness.

"Yes, it's really wonderful to see," she said hypocritically, "the man, his hands, the rope . . ." She was thinking of the guldens that he had sacrificed and that she bitterly needed at home. "You have really done it marvelously, Franzl."

"Right! Haven't I?" cried Franz joyfully. "Dr. Luser said so too, when he was here not long ago with his wife, Agatha. He thought, though, that the light should be brighter. And the pictures, he said, should be more accurate and have more detail—like photographs. Yes, if I could only use photographs! But for that copper would have to be transparent!"

He had replaced the disk with another one, which showed a ball-throwing Chinese. He had adapted the twelve pictures from Stampfer's Stroboscope and painted them in colors on glass. Anna asked, as casually as if she didn't really care to hear the answer: "And now what can you do with it?"

"Yes, of course, what can one do with it?" repeated Lieutenant Uchatius. He hesitated. "Well . . . one can show it around . . . exhibit it . . . to someone who might be interested in it . . . to General Hauslaab, for example . . ."

Hadn't she felt, long before, what was important to Franz? He wanted to show the General what he could do. Anna Uchatius suddenly understood that many people act under a compulsion to prove their worth to others. Was Franz one of them? She saw the rapture in his tense features. Or was it simply honest joy in this plaything?

The question nagged at her while she made an effort to admire the ball-throwing Chinese projected onto the wall.

Lieutenant Uchatius had had the presumption to invite
Artillery General Franz Baron von Hauslaab, "most humbly,
to an exhibition of moving pictures projected on the wall."
Scheyer, acting out of old friendship, had undertaken to
convey the invitation.

The General announced that he would come on a certain
Tuesday, postponed the visit until Thursday, then until a
week later. Finally he sat, as if enthroned, on the chair that
Anna had recently used. Scheyer stood respectfully beside
him, and Uchatius cranked as if his life depended on it.

"Ah," said Hauslaab after a while, remembering the ball-
thrower from his experience with Stampfer, "are only Chinese suitable for this novelty?" He laughed at his own
remark. "I had really hoped to be able, by this means, to
observe the impact of artillery shells. I see now, on the
contrary, . . ."

Scheyer, who was familiar with all the difficulties that
Uchatius had overcome, was exasperated again by the provocative vehemence with which the General—far from
speaking a single word of appreciation—enjoyed tormenting
the defenseless Lieutenant.

"And one more thing, gentlemen," rasped Hauslaab in
conclusion; "the picture should be brighter. And, besides,
other pictures are needed. And this flickering, if a man were
exposed to it long enough, would certainly drive him crazy."
Then, with the arrogance he had practiced for years, he
turned to Uchatius. "And you, Lieutenant, take this advice:
you should produce cannon that destroy life, not toy cannon"
—he pointed to the projecting tube of the apparatus—"that
call life forth—even though only on the wall and in this
inadequate way. Otherwise I shall be driven to the conclusion
that you have missed your calling. Even that is possible."

This time Anna was really in despair. While she prepared
the evening meal, of a frugality suitable to their slender purse,
she kept glancing through the half-open door into the living

room, and she had to struggle to keep back her tears. This was the third evening that Franz had sat immovably on the sofa, his head supported heavily on his arm. On his forehead lay that dark cloud that she feared more than anything else. Would his depression reach the point where it would make him incapable of work—as it had done some years before?

She had tried to convince Franz that the offensive General was just one of those cynical know-it-alls who can't do anything remarkable themselves and therefore take pleasure in disparaging the achievements of others.

And what had Franz answered?

"You too were disappointed, Anna. Admit it!"

Then, in his self-tormenting way, he quoted that stupid question of hers that she thought he had failed to hear—"Is that all there is?"—and he wouldn't believe her reassurances. He squeezed his bitterness into her own words: "After all, what *can* I do with the thing?" To avoid having to answer, she had fled to the kitchen.

She had been lurking there ever since. How much longer could this ghastly game go on?

A vigorous knocking at the front door broke through her anxious brooding. In the corridor stood a well-groomed, imposing man, who, flourishing his high silk hat with irresistible charm, said: "I am Ludwig Döbler. Döbler! A name . . . a concept! Prestidigitator . . . magician and conjurer of worldwide renown!" He bowed with a gesture that he had practiced with a large audience in mind. "May I speak to Lieutenant Franz Uchatius?"

Anna, glad of the distraction, led the extraordinary man into the living room.

"Monsieur! Lieutenant! I have heard about your apparatus. Magnifique! Wunderbar! A certain Dr. Luser told me about it—a charming man, by the way, and a most impressive expert in the field of photography! To him was granted the extraordinary honor of participating in one of your performances. He is overflowing with enthusiasm! So am I! I want to acquire your apparatus. I offer you a hundred guldens for it!"

Anna was beaming behind the stranger's broad back. She was a practical woman. The offer not only confirmed the importance of Franz's four years of stubborn work but also made a welcome contribution to the hard-pressed household. Franz himself, uncertain of the value of his achievement, was on the point of refusing. But the showman, accustomed to talking down all opposition, came to Anna's help.

"Oh, please, sir, do not say no! At least do not say no until you have heard me to the end. You are not relinquishing the apparatus to one who is unworthy of it, but to Ludwig Döbler." His broad gestures were again suitable to a gigantic hall. "As I said, the name is—a concept! My mist-pictures arouse storms of enthusiasm. I do not know whether you have ever had the pleasure of admiring them. Only Daguerre himself—in his Diorama—has approached such quality. You, Lieutenant, being of the profession, so to speak, certainly know the secret: a double projector. While one picture is fading out, the other appears through the second objective. A tremendous success! Satisfaction for the curious crowd! Mist-pictures: so people call them. It's a stale name and can easily be misunderstood. I call them Dissolving Views! Scintillating! And now, as the completion of my program, no, rather as the climax of my unique exhibitions: your projected moving pictures. I make publicity for you and pay you a hundred guldens besides. The chance of a lifetime! Shake hands on it!"

But Franz Uchatius did not shake hands on it. To Anna's displeasure, he insisted that Prestidigitator Döbler should first be convinced of the quality of his pictures.

The next day Döbler drove up to the barracks in his own carriage, got out of it with masterly grace, as if he were Prince Metternich himself, and took up a grand pose on the accustomed chair. He declared the exhibition to be, alternately, "exquisite" and "fulminating."

Before Uchatius realized what was happening, his projector had been wrapped in a soft, thick quilt. With the greatest caution the magician himself carried the bundle to his carriage and stowed it away there as if it were a treasure.

Uchatius had not even looked after him; he simply stared at the spot where the apparatus had been and where now a hundred guldens lay. A painful feeling of conflict arose in him. He suddenly seemed base to himself—like a mother who has sold her child.

At the same moment he decided to atone for his betrayal. He would build a new apparatus—improved, perfected. He would replace the flickering oil lamp with a Drummond limelight; increase the diameter of the picture, if possible, to six feet; modify the movement of the picture disk, so that each picture would really stand still while it was being projected on the wall. And then, especially, the quality of the pictures must be greatly improved. General Hauslaab was no doubt right about that, for Luser had said the same.

Meanwhile Döbler's horses were drawing his carriage carefully, at a discreet pace, toward the city. The magician, sunk back into a corner in a theatrical pose, smiled contentedly. He was happy to have acquired the apparatus for a mere hundred guldens. Perhaps he would have smiled even more broadly if he had known that for the next ten years he would tour the capitals of Europe with this apparatus and earn a fortune with it.

On the other hand, it might have sobered him if he had had any idea that the apparatus he was carrying with him was, in all essentials, the first cinematographic projector, that not millions, but billions, would some day be made with its successors, and that he would be the first to present this treasure to the world.

But then, in 1845, no one thought of such a thing. There was no such word as "cinematography."

6.

MINUTES SHRINK TO SECONDS

SPURRED on by Daguerre's triumph, proclaimed to the world by François Arago on January 7, 1839, many men suddenly maintained that they had been working on the same problem for a long time—and not without success. If anyone had a right to make this claim, it was William Fox Talbot, a rich and independent scholar, who, on his sleepy family estate, Lacock Abbey in Wiltshire, England, had been carrying out photographic experiments.

Talbot had got into photography in the usual way—by failing in his attempts, with the help of a camera obscura, to draw the beautiful scenes encountered in his travels. He then remembered, from his studies at Trinity College, Cambridge, that the silver salts are sensitive to light. Having more confidence in chemistry than in his own dexterity, he began experimenting. He had obtained his best results, so far, by coating paper with table salt (sodium chloride), brushing it with a solution of silver nitrate (thereby producing a layer of silver chloride), and bathing it, after exposure, in a solution of silver nitrate. Such paper was good for making photographic profiles—contact prints—of lace, leaves, and other flat objects, but it was not satisfactory for use in the camera obscura: an exposure of a full hour left on the paper only a faint impression of an object outlined against the bright sky.

Talbot continued his experiments, and in August 1835, by washing his paper alternately with sodium chloride and silver nitrate, and by exposing it while it was still damp, he succeeded in taking a picture, from the inside of his home, of a latticed window through which the bright daylight streamed. The picture was what we now call a negative; that is, the lights and darks were reversed, the light sky appearing dark, the dark lattice appearing light. Talbot fixed it with a concentrated solution of sodium chloride. This, the first photograph on paper, can still be seen in the Science Museum, South Kensington, London.

He did not make his process known, however, until Arago had told the world about the Daguerreotype. Talbot then informed the Royal Society, in London, of his results, and insisted that the credit for making the first photographs belonged to him. On February 20, 1839, being stubborn and energetic, he sent a similar message to Professor Biot of the French Academy of Sciences; and he added that he now used a much better means of fixing the image than Daguerre did. But he kept that means a secret.

He knew that he would soon have to make it known, however, for he realized that he could neither keep secret nor claim for himself a means that had really been known for twenty years. After Talbot's report to the Royal Society, Sir John Herschel had reminded him that sodium thiosulphate (often known as "hypo"), which he—Sir John—had discovered twenty years before, dissolves the silver salts. Since there had been no demand for sodium thiosulphate in 1819, Sir John's observation had nearly been forgotten—or, rather, like many another discovery, it had had to wait until the time was ripe for it.

Daguerre smiled when Biot showed him Talbot's letter. "The priority of my invention," he said, "was demonstrated to all the world by Arago's address to the Academy." He was glad to learn, a little later, that sodium thiosulphate was a better fixing agent than the table salt that he had been using.

Daguerre considered himself really justified in smiling at Talbot's process: paper—what a material to work with, compared with his durable metal plate! No, his method would not be displaced by this innovation—especially when one considered Talbot's much longer exposure time. Even a daguerreotype called for great patience!

John William Draper, Professor of Chemistry and Physiology at the University of the City of New York (now named New York University), extorted such patience from those who sat for his portraits. Excited by the description of the new daguerreotype process given him by his colleague Samuel F. B. Morse, he began, soon after Morse's return to New York late in 1839, to experiment and to try to make daguerreotype portraits. Finally, on the roof of his house, by filtering the sunlight through a tank of blue-tinted water (to block the light waves that produced the most heat), coating the sitter's face heavily with white powder, holding her head fixed in a clamp, and using a plate fumed with both iodine and bromine, he obtained, in the spring of 1840, a satisfactory daguerreotype portrait of his sister. (The water tank and the white powder soon proved to be unnecessary.)

This early photographic portrait of a human being aroused general admiration and delight. Encouraged by this success, Draper and Morse set up, on the roof of the university building, the first photographic portrait studio in the world. The simplest picture cost five dollars. The most distinguished New Yorkers, undeterred by the need of holding out for a long time in torturing immobility, crowded into the studio.

But the exposure time must be shortened! That was clear to everyone.

There were two ways to do it: through optics and through chemistry. Petzval had just gone the first way: he had cut Daguerre's exposure time to a sixteenth of what it had been, but his objectives were not yet generally available. (It took Voigtländer ten years, beginning in this same year, 1840, to produce the first 1,500 of them.)

Draper in America, Goddard in England, and Kratochwila and the Natterer brothers in Vienna, had more confidence in chemistry: they were exposing the silver layer of the metal plates to the fumes of both bromine and iodine and thereby cut the exposure time to a fourth of what it had been. Every minute of Daguerre's exposures was shrinking to a second.

This work improved Daguerre's process but neither changed its principle nor disturbed its pre-eminence. Its devotees were troubled, however, by the use of mercury vapor as a developer, which required considerable skill and was dangerous to health. No one could guess how many people, in the secrecy of their darkrooms, had tried to solve this problem by substituting a harmless bath for the dangerous vapor.

In the meantime Talbot had come forward again. In 1840 he had made two important discoveries: that silver iodide, in the presence of gallic acid and silver nitrate, was much more sensitive to light than silver chloride; and that there was no need to expose the silver-iodide paper in the camera obscura until a clear image appeared, for an image that was hardly visible or even invisible (what we now call a latent image) could be developed to a full image with additional gallic acid and silver nitrate. He no longer needed to expose his paper for an hour; he could take a picture in only half a minute.

It was true that the image he obtained on paper in his camera obscura was a negative, not, like the Daguerreotype, a positive; but the way to get a positive was obvious. He impregnated his paper negative with wax to make the light parts of it translucent, exposed through it another sheet of light-sensitive paper, and developed the second sheet. He then had what he wanted: a positive picture, in which the lights and darks corresponded to those of the scene he had photographed. He could, moreover, make as many such positive pictures—prints we now call them—as he wanted. He soon discovered that paper coated with silver chloride was the best for such prints.

Talbot was the first man who used a negative for making positive prints. All later black-and-white photography is based on his work. When he announced his new process, which he called the Calotype, on February 8, 1841, Daguerre's throne began to wobble.

The Calotype process was capable of producing very fine pictures: D. O. Hill of Edinburgh, as early as 1843, turned out Calotype portraits that are still considered among the finest photographic portraits ever made. Yet the process never became so popular as the Daguerreotype, perhaps because Talbot was unreasonable: he prosecuted all who, by using his process, violated his rights as inventor. Only when the President of the Royal Society persuaded him to take a gentler, more progressive attitude did he release his technique for non-commercial purposes. By the time that happened, however, other processes were being developed (many men were working on the problem), and it was not the Calotype that replaced Daguerre's process.

The first of the two innovations that made the Daguerreotype obsolete was introduced, ironically, by a relative of that Nicéphore Niepce who had once been Daguerre's partner and whom many insisted on regarding as the real father of photography.

The Calotype had one disadvantage: the fibrous structure of the paper negative showed on the positive print. Claude Niepce de Saint-Victor adopted, as the base of the light-sensitive coating, a substance that, being transparent, did not have to be waxed and that did not, like paper, have a visible structure: he adopted glass. His problem was then to find a suitable substance for the coating: something that would hold the light-sensitive silver salts, would be chemically innocuous, and would stick to smooth glass so firmly that it would not come loose even during development. He tried starch paste, albumen (eggwhite), gelatin, and innumerable other materials. In 1847 he adopted albumen. His plates produced fine negatives, but they were slow and required long exposures.

He was not the only one who thought that it could not be the final solution.

Gustave Le Gray, a French painter, on the advice of a friend, a certain Poitevin, had dedicated himself to the development of photography. He published what he had learned, in June 1850, in a pamphlet entitled *Photography on Glass and Paper*, in which he called attention, for the first time, to the usefulness of collodion in photography. When exposed to air, collodion—a solution of nitrocellulose in a mixture of alcohol and ether—dries very quickly to a thin skin. It had long been used by physicians to seal wounds. According to Le Gray, collodion was the best carrier of the light-sensitive silver salts.

The next year, 1851, Le Gray received a letter about his use of collodion. It bore an Austrian stamp, was postmarked in Vienna, and was written in miserable French:

"Sir: I have been following the development of photography since its beginning, in all departments, at home and abroad. I have also read your pamphlet. Following its advice, I have tried to produce a collodion plate. You are said to be an artist, and perhaps that is the reason for the confusion; in any case, one cannot do practical work by following your instructions. Read the latest issue of the English journal *The Chemist*, and you will be surprised to find there how simply F. S. Archer describes what seems to be the same process. I should be greatly interested in knowing whether his technique is really the same as yours."

In the lower right corner, rather hard to make out, was the name: Dr. Gerhardt Luser.

Le Gray, who had thought he was near the goal of his dreams, who intended to inherit Daguerre's pre-eminence, was shocked by Luser's letter. He immediately disputed Archer's priority in the invention of the collodion process. At the end of their tedious, nerve-wracking struggle, when he had paid more than his last penny to his lawyer, Le Gray emigrated to Egypt as a teacher of drawing. Many thought that he was really fleeing from his creditors.

And Archer, his victorious but embittered opponent? Archer died in poverty six years after the announcement of his process, leaving his wife and children in the severest distress. Grateful young devotees of photography took up a collection for them to soften both their bitterest need and the injustice they felt. Only then did the British government grant a yearly pension of fifty pounds to the children of the "discoverer of a scientific process of great value to the nation, from which he himself had drawn no benefit."

Poitevin, reporting Archer's fate to his friend Le Gray, who was still in Egypt, added: "As you know, I think your wet-collodion process is just about the most troublesome that any photographer could imagine: a process in which the collodion-coated plate has to be sensitized in the silver bath just before the exposure, so that it can be put into the camera wet, and after the exposure has to be developed as soon as possible, before the coating dries. Despite these difficulties, it not only is the best process now, but probably will be the best for a long time. It has quickly displaced the process for which Daguerre received incomparably greater thanks. If you are reasonable, the thought that your process is successful and valuable will console you." The unhappy Le Gray, soon afterward, fell from his horse and died of his injuries.

While Le Gray and Archer were disputing each other's claims, their wet-collodion process (for which Archer is now generally given the credit) had been making its way all over the civilized world and becoming the standard photographic process. Ardent photographers were not deterred by its inconvenience and difficulty, and they used it for amazingly fine and historically valuable work.

In 1855, only a few years after Archer's invention, Roger Fenton was sent out from London to photograph scenes of the Crimean War. Working with a closed wagon clearly labeled PHOTOGRAPHIC VAN, he finished 350 wet-collodion negatives and brought them back to England.

Mathew B. Brady, one of the first pupils of Samuel Morse's school of photography and long America's leading daguerreotypist, being famous for his superior portraits of well-known persons (he won a medal at the London exhibition of 1851), adopted the wet-collodion process in time to make magnificent use of it during the Civil War. Traveling with a rolling darkroom (an enclosed wagon that the soldiers called his "What-is-it?"), training and supervising teams of photographers, and taking pictures himself in the line of battle, he produced thousands of wet-collodion negatives of great historical importance.

Brady took his work very seriously. "From the first," he said late in his life, "I regarded myself as under obligation to my country to preserve the faces of its historical men and women. . . . The camera is the eye of history; you must never make bad pictures."

The devotees of photography experimented and experimented, but the wet-collodion process, with all its disadvantages, remained predominant for almost a generation. Among those disadvantages was the necessity of a portable darkroom, from which the photographer could never stray very far—a tent or closed wagon providing the darkness in which he could prepare the wet plate just before the exposure and develop it right afterward. A troublesome business!

Freeing photographers from that burden was the unforgettable achievement of Richard Leach Maddox, an Englishman. His stubborn labor of twenty years had used up all the savings he had accumulated during his work as a physician in Constantinople when, on September 8, 1871, in the *British Journal of Photography*, he made public the first results of his experiments. Maddox used gelatin as the carrier and silver bromide as the light-sensitive salt. He spread this emulsion on glass plates and let it dry completely. Such dry plates, as they were called, could be kept, without deterioration, in plate-holders or in opaque paper and could still be developed long after exposure. Photographers could now wait until they were home to develop their plates with alkaline pyrogallol, hydrochinone, or other chemicals and to fix them with sodium thiosulphate.

At first photographers prepared their own dry plates—a task requiring great care and skill. The first commercial dry plates appeared on the English market in 1877. Everyone admitted that they were much more convenient than the collodion plate, but photographers were slow to accept them as better in other ways. Their great sensitivity was, strange to say, regarded at first as a fault. They were about ten times as fast as wet-collodion plates, and photographers were always over-exposing their pictures. It was nearly five years before photographers got used to them and admitted that they were an improvement in anything but convenience.

The development of photography, in its essentials, was thereby finished. Daguerre, who used, for his metal plates, the sensitivity to light of the silver salts (discovered by Schulze), was followed by Talbot with his paper negative-positive process, by Niepce de Saint-Victor with his glass plate, by Archer with his effective but troublesome wet-collodion process, and now by Maddox with his dry gelatin emulsion. How little his negatives, from which one could make as many prints as one wanted on light-sensitive paper, had in common with Daguerre's cumbersome metal plates!

Yet Maddox, accustomed to rash proposals and constant

innovation in photography, never suspected that his dry plate covered with gelatin and silver bromide would give photography its final form. He did not patent his process. The little neighborhood photographer in the side street of a small town profited more by it than Maddox himself.

After defeat in the Franco-Prussian War, after the miseries and deprivations suffered during the siege of the city, the life of Paris was returning to its usual carefree ways. One day in the spring of 1878 the golden light of the sun cast a spell on the ancient splendor of the boulevards, and the Parisians' love of life foamed again through the city, as if everything evil were forgotten. In the gay crowd of idlers one man stood out: a careworn old man who sat in front of the café on the Boulevard des Capucines and stared sullenly at the dregs of his stingy glass of absinthe.

For all his appearance, the good fellow might not be very old, thought the young man opposite him, who lolled on the only free chair he had found. He cast a sidelong glance at the man's high forehead, at his plump nose, which, like a potato, hung between his sagging cheeks above an unkempt beard. Perhaps the fellow was only a little over fifty! These people from the country, worn out by hard work, always looked older than they were.

The old man, leaning, in peasant style, on the gnarled stick clamped between his knees, paid no attention to the sunshine or to the turmoil of the city and certainly not to the thoughts of the young man. He did not even raise his head when a shadow fell on the table. The shadow belonged to a dandified man who carried over his shoulder a mighty tripod to which a massive camera was attached.

"Hey, Grandpa, how about a picture?" Since the old man didn't even twitch an eyelash, the stranger went on talking. "A photograph is the most beautiful souvenir you can take home to your loved ones. A souvenir of Paris! A remembrance that will last forever . . ."

"Go to the devil!"

"Oh la la!" cried the smart gentleman, nevertheless setting up his apparatus. "You will yet be grateful to me! There's nothing like this in the provinces."

"Go to the devil, I said!" snarled the bearded one. His tone of voice attracted the attention of those around him.

The photographer could not give up. "Sir, it's the opportunity of a lifetime! No daguerreotype, no tinplate! From me you can order copies on paper, as many as you want—one for each acquaintance. I work with the latest process—with original English dry plates."

The old man's gnarled stick whirled in the air. "I am going to count to three. After that you can drag away the remains of your box—if you are still able to. One . . . two . . ."

The people at the next tables had sprung up; the young man leaned forward and tried to calm the old man. "Really, mon père, the gentleman has no evil intentions. He assumes that you come from the provinces, and visitors from the provinces always like to have their pictures taken. That's taken for granted, isn't it, sir?"

But the photographer, to whom the old man had seemed too eager to carry out his threat, had suddenly disappeared, and the old man was again sitting quietly on his chair, his stick between his knees, looking older than before.

In front of the café people were again going back and forth on the sidewalk; conversation at the tables revived; the dispute was forgotten. Parisians had more to remember than such a trifling incident.

Suddenly the old man's eyes—unusually penetrating, surprisingly clear eyes—were directed across the table. "Perhaps I did not behave well, sir—at least in your opinion. I think I should explain myself."

Under his strangely compelling gaze the young man merely shrugged.

"I do come from the provinces; that is right. I was born

at Conflans, in the department of the Sarthe. But I studied here in Paris—chemistry and mechanics—at the Central School of Arts and Handicrafts. It was just the time when Mr. Daguerre excited the world with his remarkable invention. Is it any wonder that I was among his disciples? Later, when I was working as civil engineer at the state salt mines, I was already going my own way in photography. Do you know that my daguerreotype plates, which I had treated with copper sulphate, provided the first photographic intaglio plates that could be used on a printing press? The process was presented to the Academy of Sciences in 1848."

He looked for a few seconds into two wide-open, astonished eyes.

"But that was only a beginning, by today's standards—a modest beginning. For a photochemical process of engraving gold-plated metal plates I received the silver medal of the Society for the Encouragement of the Arts. Do you want to hear more? You can take my word for it: it went on like that."

The young man looked surprised rather than convinced.

"Perhaps I was never envied so much as when I was awarded the prize of the Duke of Luynes for a photographic printing process using carbon: 10,000 francs! At that time I had given up my position in Lyon and had come back to Paris. I suppose that many people, with that capital, would have embarked on a carefree life . . ."

His gaze wandered over the passing idlers and then returned to the young man. "It was about that time that Niepce de Saint-Victor—I don't know whether the name means anything to you—introduced the glass plate as the base of the light-sensitive coating. The trouble was that we didn't have the right material for that coating . . ."

He hesitated as if he had come to a critical point, or perhaps it was only the unconcealed amazement of the other that irritated him.

"Thirty years have passed since then—almost a lifetime!

In those days I threw myself into that problem with a confidence, a fanaticism, that I simply don't understand today. I swore by gelatin as the coating; only gelatin would do. I sacrificed everything to that idea—my days, my nights, my abilities, my not inconsiderable capital . . ."

"And . . .?"

"And? Nothing came of it all. I was a beggar when I left Paris and took over the direction of a glass works in the provinces. What else was left? The last thing that I did for photography was to call the attention of a friend, Gustave Le Gray, to the most important question: the coating, the carrier of the light-sensitive salts. Le Gray then hit upon that unfortunate collodion process. He is dead . . . the collodion process is dead . . . Let's forget all that."

"And your gelatin?" asked the young man, eager, sincerely interested.

"You have just heard! The brilliantined gentleman wanted to take my picture on an 'original English dry plate'! But why should you know that the essential thing in this latest photographic process is gelatin—*my* gelatin!" He shoved his knobby nose far over the table. "That's easy to say. But what's behind those words—for me, for my life? Think now! If I had reached that time just an inch farther into the cupboard, where the jars of hydrochinone, ferrous oxalate, ferrous sulphate, and potassium oxalate stood, I should have saved all our black-and-white artists from a detour that led them astray for nearly three decades. Just one inch! What's one inch, young man? That was all that separated me then from the success of all my efforts, from worldwide fame, perhaps from riches! Can you feel what it means to miss success by just one inch?"

"I call it tough luck!"

The stranger played with the knob of his stick and regarded him closely. "Today it's a waste of time, of course, to ask whether it was bad luck that I didn't reach farther into the cupboard or whether I simply forgot that silver iodide and gallic acid behave badly in combination with gelatin. The chance is gone." He wiped his flat hand over the table as if he were brushing away a shadow, then looked up again. "And now along comes that fellow and wants to photograph me on a gelatin plate—me, the tired old grandpa from the country—to provide a lasting souvenir for a couple of simple-minded peasant boys . . ." The old man sank back in his chair and leaned again on his stick, his gaze on his empty glass. Now he seemed to be a man like all the others— only more sullen, more miserable, more insignificant.

The young man facing him felt the need to say something conciliatory, something that would express his sympathy. "Can I do anything for you?" he asked, and he felt at once how ridiculous his offer was.

But the old man surprised him. "Yes!" he answered promptly. And then it sounded like a pleading: "Say that you understand why I behaved as I did a while ago."

The young man could only nod at first. A little later he declared: "Your life sounds like a novel, Mr. . . ."

"Poitevin is my name—Alphonse Louis Poitevin."

7.

CANNON OR CAMERA?

ARCHDUKE Wilhelm, as General Inspector of the Imperial Austrian Army, was preparing reports on the higher officers. One of them, Colonel Uchatius, had been troubling his mind for some time. The Colonel had certainly accomplished extraordinary things for Austria. There was the part he had played in the creation of the Arsenal. And he had so many brilliant ideas! During the siege of Venice, in 1848, this Uchatius had arranged the first air attack in the history of the world! Yet, the Archduke told himself, all those achievements could not conceal the fact that the man was now almost sixty years old and that, even if he felt well at the moment, he had recently, because of nervous agitation, been unfit for service for four months. The Archduke remembered also that Uchatius was said to have suffered from melancholia for almost a year when he was still an artilleryman—an incapacity that had recently been tactlessly rubbed under his, the Archduke's, nose because he was considered the Colonel's protector. That too, of course, had to be taken into account.

The Archduke was aware that what he wrote would amount to a final judgment of a worthy man for whom he had uncommon sympathy, that it would determine the end of a career that had been full of good will, great ability, and tireless work.

It was already getting dark when he finally took up his pen. "This very deserving staff officer, distinguished in his specialty, is already too advanced in age to be able to assert a claim to promotion." The Archduke considered a while. Perhaps he was too severe. In order to soften his judgment, he added: "I permit myself, nevertheless, to recommend most warmly that he be treated with the utmost consideration." With a deep sigh he put his pen down.

Because of this recommendation, Colonel Uchatius, in 1871, despite his sixty years, was made Commandant of the Ordnance Works in the Vienna Arsenal. In the opinion of many, even of those who had no ill will for him, that was more than he had a right to expect—for he was, they thought, mere scrap iron.

His rise began hardly a year later. It was a meteoric rise, a rise that carried him not only to the highest honors of the Austro-Hungarian Dual Monarchy but to world significance and world fame.

A piece of metal was the cause. The Archduke, returning from a trip to Russia, brought home with him a piece of bronze and handed it over to his confidant, Colonel Uchatius.

"That looks like a good metal for cannon," he said.

Uchatius took the remark as an order. Retiring into his laboratory, he began to analyze the metal chemically and test it mechanically. And then he took the decisive step: he himself reached for the crucible. In his stubborn, dogged way he searched for the alloy that Archduke Wilhelm expected of him, that Austria needed. Those around him, accustomed though they were to his unsurpassable capacity for work, saw new marvels. Oblivious of the difference between day and night, he devised new alloys, cast them, tested them, and finally, by techniques devised by him for this purpose, compressed them.

So, with unprecedented persistence, he developed an alloy that satisfied his high demands.

"Uchatius bronze!" exclaimed Archduke Wilhelm happily when he was convinced, by the laboratory tests, of the outstanding quality of the material. "They will all have to admit, Uchatius, that the best metal for cannon is named after you."

The final decision depended, however, on the trial firings. These, which took place in September 1873, gave such satisfactory results that the problem seemed to be solved. Archduke Wilhelm and the Minister of War succeeded, against the wishes of the Military Committee under its hostile chairman, in having the Uchatius bronze adopted.

For a fraction of a second—as measured in world history—the power of the Dual Monarchy rose.

In the game played by the Great Powers, in which millions in armament capital—and millions of human lives—were at stake, cannon were decisive—cannon and the metal of which they were made. Who had such metal? England was producing Bessemer steel; Germany was producing Krupp cast steel cannon; France had been pushed into the background by its defeat in the Franco-Prussian War; the recently united Italy was too young; Russia had little heavy industry. It was Austria's most burning ambition to demonstrate its importance in the world by producing its own metal for cannon.

The sickly boy who had grown up in modest circumstances helped the monarchy to achieve its goal and thereby become overnight a decisive figure in the politics of the Great Powers. The rulers of the Dual Monarchy thanked this Uchatius in their usual way: they made him a major-general and, hardly a year later, a lieutenant field marshal; Emperor Franz Josef bestowed on him the Commander's Cross of the Order of Saint Stephen, gave him the title of Privy Councilor, and made him a baron—this last being, according to the social ideas of the time, a very special distinction.

When the Order of the Iron Crown, Second Class, which brought with it a lifelong annual pension of two thousand guldens, was bestowed on him, Frau Anna showed a bitter-sweet smile. She thought of the theatrical magician who once, with a hundred guldens, had balanced her household budget. Wondering whether Franz remembered, she glanced at him. He was looking grave—as he usually did lately. He was too grave, and that disturbed her.

Two days later, however, there was no doubt that he did remember. Alfried von Winter, a close friend, was there, and they had just had supper.

"Weren't you once interested in this, Franz?" asked Winter as he handed him a copy of the *Scientific American*. He pointed out an article illustrated with many pictures of a galloping horse.

Uchatius read how, in Palo Alto, California, a photographer named Eadweard Muybridge had invented a way of breaking up a rapid continuous movement into a series of still shots. Even though he used the clumsy wet-collodion process, Muybridge, by a series of instantaneous exposures made with twenty-four cameras set up in a row, had succeeded in fixing the successive phases of a galloping horse's movement. He had proved that a galloping horse, during each cycle of its gallop, has all four feet off the ground for a fraction of a second; and he had shown how motion could be analyzed and studied by means of photography.

"Right!" said Uchatius, putting down the magazine, a mild melancholy showing in his eyes as he looked into the distance. "I wanted such serial photographs for my projector, but there was no way to get them in those days."

"Didn't you ever work at it any more?"

"Oh, for a while. Some years after I sold my first apparatus for a hundred guldens, I finished a new and improved one, with limelight. The pictures were stationary, with a projection lens in front of each, and it was the light that revolved, passing each picture in turn. With that apparatus the pictures remained quiet on the wall. I even presented a report on it to the Academy of Sciences."

"And then?"

Uchatius shrugged. "My military duties took all my time. Nothing remained but the tender affection that one always feels for one's first love—or one's first hobby." With a gesture of fatigue and resignation he seemed to dismiss the past. "But pictures like these"—he pointed to the magazine—"I could have used. Then, perhaps, I should not have been enticed away so easily, not even by bronze!" After a moment he added softly: "I'd like to see such a series of pictures sometime—at least see them."

Winter, glad of a chance to dispel his friend's gloom, said brightly: "That can certainly not be much of a problem! We simply have to write to this Muybridge and ask him to lend us one of his series. If he didn't feel flattered by the interest of others, he would certainly be the first such inventor."

"Do you really think so?" asked Uchatius. The gleam in his eyes conjured forth on his symmetrical, manly features an expression that many—especially Anna—had missed for a long time. His friend decided to do all he could to get hold of such pictures, even if he had to bring them from America himself.

Not long afterward Uchatius was reminded again of his experiments, of his hobby.

It was a spring evening, and he was sitting for Professor Sigmund L'Allemand, who was even better known as a portrait painter, if that was possible, than as a battle painter. The Professor's brush was to keep alive for later generations the memory of Baron von Uchatius. In the compulsory leisure of sitting still the Lieutenant Field Marshal was able to think about the trouble he had been having with the casting of a 28-centimeter coastal gun. His opponents would regard the success of this gun as the final, decisive proof of the value of the Uchatius bronze. The Field Marshal was in a bad humor.

He was torn out of his ugly mood by a little man who, supporting himself on a cane, limped unexpectedly into the studio and murmured, "Pardon me!"

L'Allemand became unfriendly: "Really, Doctor, how can you . . .?"

But the old gentleman, unconcerned, walked stiffly up to Uchatius. "You don't seem to recognize me, Your Excellency. I am Luser, Dr. Luser."

"Luser? Luser?"

The painter felt obliged to intervene. "Dr. Luser is kind enough to photograph some of my pictures for a catalogue. We agreed to do it today. But, Doctor"—he clearly could not conceal his displeasure—"we agreed on a later hour, after His Excellency's sitting is finished."

"That is just why I am here now." The unruffled cheerfulness and glowing satisfaction of the old man were irresistible. "I did not want to let slip the opportunity to renew our acquaintance, Your Excellency. Our common interest in photography brought us together once upon a time. But that was a long, long time ago. You then gave me the pleasure of seeing the first living pictures."

And then the Field Marshal remembered him. Yes, it was the same Dr. Luser who had brought about the sale of his apparatus to Döbler, the showman.

"Are you still working on this problem?" asked Dr. Luser.

No, answered Uchatius, he had given up his experiments; he had not had time for them—to his great regret.

"That's too bad!" exclaimed Dr. Luser.

"Yes, too bad!" repeated Uchatius, and Luser did not suspect how sincerely, at the moment, he meant this.

Professor L'Allemand, suddenly feeling shoved aside, laid

down his palette. The odd pair of men, surprisingly united by a mysterious bond, captivated his artist's eye: the famous officer with the unmistakable shadows of spiritual suffering on his slack, tired features, and the obscure little man whose rosy old cheeks glowed with deep inner contentment.

"But certainly you still take pictures, Your Excellency!"

No, said Uchatius regretfully, even for that he had no time; but as soon as he could free himself of the worst difficulties in the Arsenal, he wanted to devote himself wholeheartedly to this new art. For some time he had been eager to do so. Through a friend he had recently received some instantaneous pictures—exposed for mere fractions of a second —that inspired him to imitate them. They were the work of a certain Muybridge. Well, the pictures would just have to wait in a drawer for a more favorable time. Did Luser know Muybridge?

"Muybridge!" Dr. Luser excitedly brandished his cane. "This year, with all the drums of publicity booming, Muybridge has been traveling all over Europe. In Berlin, at the Urania, he even exhibited his pictures to Helmholtz, Siemens, Menzel, and Moltke. But he is not the only one who is trying serial pictures." Dr. Luser, at ease, talked on as if nothing at that moment could interest the officer more. Neither man seemed to remember the artist. "There is also Jules Janssen, the astronomer, who photographed the transit of Venus, and Marey, also French, a physiologist, who has built a sort of photographic rifle. It takes automatic serial pictures—twelve pictures a second—and is superior, certainly superior, to Muybridge's method. You simply have to aim it at the object! Muybridge is in Paris right now, I have heard, working with Marey. Oh, yes, and there's Anschütz, Ottomar Anschütz, from Lissa, near Posen. He's probably about thirty-five years old. Just think what we can still expect from him! He is said to produce extraordinary serial pictures—little works of art!"

"You are well informed in this field, Dr. Luser!"

Luser beamed like the sun in May. "Photography," he said, "is my passion! And I was unusually lucky: my passion was also my profession. I had a position in the Military Geographic Institute. Who knows how many of the General Staff maps that you have handled were printed with my photo-electrotypes? Today, of course, I am retired and enjoying my pension. Nevertheless, Your Excellency, despite my seventy-six years, I am still taking part in all the developments." He struck the floor energetically with his cane. "Black-and-white pictures no longer satisfy me. I want colored pictures. A German professor—Vogel is his name—has announced a process that seems to be very promising. I am experimenting with it."

The painter scraped the paint off his palette with a spatula and began to clear away his tools. He had finally given up the hope of being able to do any more work.

"Photography, taking pictures! Have you ever stopped to think, Your Excellency, how well this technique is adapted to the nature of mankind? Does not every human being have, slumbering within himself, an artistic impulse—which, however, not everyone can satisfy with pencil or brush? Yes, only a few can do that! But choosing a favorable spot on which to stand and a rewarding sector of the view—can't everybody do that? Today, with dry plates, with powerful objectives, with the new, simple ways of developing, everything else is pure enjoyment. What remains behind is pleasant memories, the evidence of hours passed in pleasure. So regarded, is not photography—like music, for example—an enrichment of our lives?"

"When I hear you, Dr. Luser, I could believe I was listening to a missionary—or to a hungry salesman for a dealer in photographic materials!"

"You have overlooked the third possibility, Your Excellency: you see a man who understands how to be happy in his own way."

Once more, it happened, Lieutenant Field Marshal Baron von Uchatius met the eccentric Dr. Luser. It was June 4, 1881.

In the morning, before he left his home in the headquarters building of the Arsenal, Uchatius had already given all the orders for his departure that evening. He was going to leave at six o'clock for Weidlingau, where he would spend the Pentecost holidays with his friend Winter, in order to find the relaxation that he badly needed.

At the usual time he went to the foundry, where he had the latest samples of bronze brought to him for inspection. There he met the Director of the Arsenal, a good friend, who had been present, in May, at the trials of the 28-centimeter cannon made of Uchatius bronze, and also at the stricter trial on June 1. Uchatius asked the Director if he knew the result of the recent trial. The Director, to spare his friend's feelings, simply hinted that it had turned up certain faults. These could certainly be taken care of, he added, but Uchatius's old opponent, the former Chairman of the Military Committee, who had recently been appointed Minister of War, had not been able to control his malicious tongue. "Will we live long enough," he was supposed to have asked, so that all present would hear him, "to see Uchatius finish his coast artillery?"

Uchatius was familiar with the man's malice; he would not let that spoil his day. He simply nodded and went quietly on his way. The Director looked after him; the calm with which Uchatius had taken the new disappointment surprised him, but it also stilled his anxiety.

Before Uchatius returned home at noon, he walked out in front of the Arsenal through the main entrance. And there, from a gigantic black cloth that covered a camera resting on a solid wooden tripod, appeared a bent figure that hobbled, with the aid of a cane, toward Uchatius.

It was Dr. Luser.

"I have obtained permission, Your Excellency, to take pictures here." He fumbled at his pocket.

"Very well! It's all right!" And Uchatius clearly dismissed him. But Luser was not to be lightly shaken off.

"About our last conversation," he said, "I have reflected a great deal, Your Excellency, and I have come to the following conclusion: You must resume your experiments! Absolutely! The time is ripe for them." His old man's loquacity was not daunted by Uchatius's defensive reserve. "It was a stroke of genius when you combined the magic lantern and the Stroboscope in order to present living pictures, but . . . but . . . it was too early! And I don't mean simply that there was no strong source of light then, such as we have today, or that you had to use those childish little home-made drawings. No, the reason goes deeper. Your apparatus was ahead of its time. People had hardly had time to understand that they could prepare finished pictures by mechanical means, and you, Your Excellency, already wanted to give them moving pictures!" He came up close to Uchatius and looked up with great effort. "But now your time has come! Combine your apparatus with Muybridge's serial pictures and with Edison's new incandescent lamp or the new arc light; remember Marey's rifle; improve the transport of the pictures—and you will be immortal!"

The Field Marshal's apathetic quiet seemed for a moment to sober Dr. Luser. He blinked, passed his hand hurriedly over his forehead. Hadn't he made himself understood? He began again.

"Progress, the constant struggle for the solution of the great problems, is irresistible. I was talking about that only yesterday with Agatha—my wife. In the powerful stream of progress particular problems are carried along; they appear at the surface, and then they go under, but they never sink to the bottom. They wait for the strong hand that will seize them. And that moment has come for your projected moving pictures. Take hold, Your Excellency!"

The little man, as rigid as if made of stone, was waiting for an answer. But Uchatius merely shrugged, and the movement seemed to conceal some helplessness. "If it were not for this cursed bronze and these cannon!" it seemed to say.

The tenseness of Luser's features gave way to a confidential air that Uchatius had never seen in him before. "I know," he said, "that powerful gentlemen like you have little free time. But one should always leave a little time to think of joyful things, Your Excellency. And making living pictures would be a joy for you. Who knows what we could still expect from your inventiveness!"

Then Uchatius spoke: "Perhaps I ought to have stayed with the pictures altogether, Dr. Luser. Perhaps I should have had more success, more satisfaction, with them than with this wretched bronze. I should have been able, at least, to create practical things of lasting value to mankind."

The bitter tone and the tired voice forced even the loquacious Luser to give up any idea of answering. Without a word he hobbled back to his camera and made his exposure with all an old man's fussiness. While he was packing up, however, he turned again to Uchatius. "With these new dry plates," he said, "taking pictures is pure pleasure." Finally he shouldered his tripod, with the camera on it, tried to bow, and, depending heavily on his cane, made his way toward the city, right into the sun.

Uchatius watched his silhouette, which became smaller and smaller and once remained standing. Dr. Luser must certainly have turned round, must be smiling at him, with his quiet, contented smile. Then the silhouette went on toward the sun.

The Field Marshal turned slowly round. The deep shadows of the unfriendly rough-brick building swallowed up his bent figure.

At one o'clock Franz Uchatius was dead.

In his study, during an attack of overpowering depression, he had ended his life with a bullet into his chest.

On his desk lay a note: "Forgive me, my dear ones. I cannot bear life any longer."

8.

REVOLUTION IN PHOTOGRAPHY

THE cashier of the insurance company in Rochester
(New York) counted three dollars into the narrow, boyish hand. Thin, bony fingers hastily closed on them. The
cashier was on the point of saying that the hands might be
cleaner, but he refrained; after all, the boy was not only the
victim of the Chief's temper and his fellow workers' moods
but also the one who had to do the dirtiest jobs. Besides, the
cashier liked him.

George stopped at the door. He opened his fist and made
sure that he had actually received three dollars. Then, carefully, he pushed them deep into his trousers pocket. They
were, after all, the biggest contribution to the support of a
family of four!

Had anyone here in the office ever thought of that? The
cashier, who seemed so friendly? Or the Chief, of all people?
George Eastman laughed bitterly.

It was in the year 1867. The young United States of
America still bore the traits of its founders, who had been
accustomed to taking care of themselves and making their
own way. Who concerned himself about the needy widow

with three young children? Who had worried about them
five years before, when Father Eastman had died?

The thirteen-year-old George did worry. He carried his
dollars home and prepared the frugal supper.

And then came night, which George feared because the
darkness made him feel his burden even more. The worn face
of his mother appeared before him, the sister made helpless
by poliomyelitis. He feared these nightly visions. But they
had been there yesterday, and they would be there again
tomorrow—the visions of poverty. An unlucky man who had
lost a leg or an eye could weep no more impotent bitterness
into his pillow than George. Was there no way, then, to
overcome poverty? That question tortured him.

Then, one evening, something special happened. George
was sweeping the floor and was listening with half an ear
to the cashier's conversation with a late customer. And then
he snapped up a phrase, torn out of its context, that sounded
like a commonplace in the mouth of the stranger: "Yes, if
one has learned something . . ."

That night, in the silence, the words came back to him,
filled his thoughts. Didn't they show the only way, without
money, to escape from this torturing poverty?

Two days later George was convinced: he must learn,
learn stubbornly, doggedly, in order to know more than the
others, to be superior to his surroundings. And then he would
use that superiority to go forward, to become rich—to become rich at any price. He clung desperately to this purpose;
it became the dominating motive of his life.

The friendly cashier lent him a book containing directions for writing good business letters, then a book on commercial law. And that was only the beginning. He studied in
the evening and often at night, when many youths of his age
were loafing on the streets.

Gradually, hesitatingly, successes came to him. At twenty
he was a bookkeeper earning seventy dollars a month. To
George Eastman, who had kept a family of four going on

three dollars a week, seventy dollars was a great deal of money. He began to save with the greatest strictness. But he didn't save, like others, for a faultlessly tailored suit, for a few days of leisure, or for a carefree old age. He saved for the opportunity of realizing his dream: finally becoming rich.

The opportunity came—as casually as it probably comes to many at some time in their lives, but George Eastman seized it.

An acquaintance called his attention to photography: "You mustn't think that I am the only fanatic. Everybody is doing it—and you should too, Eastman." Perhaps the man simply wanted to justify his passion. But Eastman pricked up his ears: something that was bewitching the whole world was worth paying attention to. The new art made a place for itself in Eastman's thinking, and from then on it never left him alone.

He began by inquiring about the cost of the essential equipment. It would be about a hundred dollars, the dealer declared. Eastman winced.

"For that price you will have almost ninety pounds of equipment to carry home—that is, if you can carry such a weight."

The dealer confirmed the great weight by enumerating the various articles, from the light-proof tent through the different chemicals to the heavy plates.

The price seemed too high to George Eastman. A few days later, however, he returned. The thriftiest man in Rochester, without batting an eye, paid $94.36 and gladly carried home his eighty-five or ninety pounds of equipment.

He would have paid and carried even more, for he had been thinking the situation over very thoroughly, in all its implications, and he had come to a remarkable conclusion: the more expensive the equipment, the greater the weight, the better for him! Every dollar, every pound, simply proved to him that something was wrong with this art of photography, an art to which everybody, apparently, felt drawn. How many of his contemporaries were kept away by the high price—all those, for example, who wangled their way through life, meagerly and painfully, on three dollars a week! Every dollar by which one reduced the cost would lead new hordes to photography. And then the great weight, the difficult manipulations! How many easygoing people must be frightened off by them! Photography must be made simpler, easier, and cheaper. Then one could really win over the masses—and become rich.

The idea fascinated Eastman.

He set up his first laboratory in the kitchen. Only a patient mother could overlook the long row of his bottles containing corrosive and poisonous chemicals, and even she could not always put up with the pungent and cough-inducing vapors. But George went on tirelessly boiling collodion emulsions, developing new recipes, and testing new developers—all with only one purpose: to simplify the complicated process of making photographs.

He soon saw that the new dry plate, in this respect, had been the greatest advance. It saved the photographer the trouble of taking along a small, light-proof chemical laboratory, and it got rid of a difficult procedure that not everyone could carry through. His attention was turned first, therefore, to the production of dry plates that could stand comparison with the original English products.

He was successful. His dry plates proved to be so good that he decided to make them in greater number. At night, in his mother's kitchen, he devoted himself zealously to their production—at a time when he was still working all day as a bookkeeper. His first customers appeared: relatives and acquaintances, all of whom had succumbed to the black-and-white art. Ten-dollar bills appeared in the house; then even hundred-dollar bills.

Encouraged by his success, he took time off to go to England, the home of the dry plate, in order to discover the tricks and secrets that make production not only technically sure but economically profitable. There, he found, people were very proud that both Archer, the inventor of the wet-collodion plate, and Maddox, the inventor of the dry plate, were Englishmen.

The plant manager to whom Eastman went for help served him up a special bit of news: "Maddox—whose dry plate has, after all, given photography its final form—hasn't earned a single penny by his invention. His well-wishers have taken up a collection to provide for his old age. And how was it with Archer? For a while, after his death, his followers had to take care of his indigent family. An amazing parallel between their two fates, Mr. Eastman!"

But Eastman was not amazed by anything. He simply wanted to know how to cook the purest colorless and odorless gelatin out of bones, how to make the finest emulsion of gelatin and silver bromide, and how to spread that emulsion evenly and perfectly on glass plates. As for Maddox's sad inventor's fate, let no one worry: that would never happen to him.

At home again in Rochester, he doubled his zeal. The kitchen became too small for him, and he rented a shop where he could turn out plates in large numbers. In the first year he produced $50,000 worth of dry plates.

Thousand-dollar checks were deposited to his account, and he was on the way to becoming rich. Since his work as bookkeeper hampered him, he gave it up.

He now decided that he could no longer waste his time simply making dry plates. If his enterprise was going to succeed, he must return to his original plan: he must revolutionize the whole art of photography. He must replace the whole ninety pounds of equipment by a cheap, handy camera, ready for operation, which required no expert knowledge, not even thought. And the buyer must no longer be bothered with the troublesome processing of the exposures. Eastman, in Rochester, would take care of that. The amateur photographer should, if possible, have nothing to do but press a button. "You press the button; we do the rest." That was the slogan with which he would launch his promotion campaign and his "people's camera"—the camera for the three-dollar man.

"With that I'll certainly get rich, Walker—perhaps even be a millionaire!"

"That's what I think," answered Eastman's most devoted helper, W. H. Walker, in an unusual spell of loquacity.

The execution of the plan was stopped at the outset by what seemed at first to be only a slight obstacle: the glass plate. If glass was the emulsion-carrier, one could load the camera for only one exposure at a time. That limitation would defeat his whole plan: he would not consider glass.

"So what?" said Eastman scornfully. "There are plenty of materials that can be bent or folded or rolled up—paper, for example. Talbot used paper."

A camera loaded with a rolled paper negative long enough for a hundred exposures was put on the market, but the quality of the pictures suffered too much from the fibrous structure of the paper. Eastman then (1884) produced what was called a stripping negative: a roll of paper coated with gelatin, which was stripped from the paper after development and then printed. This kind of negative was still being used when the first Kodak, a box camera taking pictures about two and a half inches in diameter, was introduced in 1888. The camera was already loaded with the negative roll when it was sold; the buyer, when he had exposed all the negative, returned the camera to the maker, who developed the roll, stripped off the gelatin, made the prints, and reloaded and returned the camera. This process, with its inconveniences, would certainly not win the market that Eastman was looking for.

The obstacle that had seemed small at first—the lack of a good flexible base for the sensitive emulsion—now began to look big.

Eastman was determined to find a way round it. There

must, he thought, be substances that were strong, transparent, and flexible. Not long after the stripping negative had been introduced, he and his helpers had already begun to experiment with gutta-percha, with finely cleft mica, with the finest cotton dissolved in cuprammonium. Nearly every day a new material was tried, and every trial failed.

The obstacle began to look insurmountable.

Eastman raged. "Do you mean to say there is no such material? Am I supposed to wait, Walker, until some chemist discovers a material that is strong, as flexible as paper, and as clear as glass?"

Walker shrugged.

"Isn't it ridiculous that an invention should be held up until some decisive step is taken in another field—a field that we haven't paid any attention to?"

"That's happened more than once," said the taciturn Walker.

"And my camera, the camera that will make it possible for the masses of the people to have fun with photography?"

Walker was satisfied with another shrug.

"And what about me? I must get rich!"

That too Walker answered with a shrug.

Not long afterward, however, he laid on his chief's desk a small disk—flexible, clear as water. He had taken it off the back of a pocket mirror that a clothing dealer in New York had packed, as an advertisement, with a suit.

Eastman's fingers played with it, cautiously at first, then excitedly.

"What is it, Walker?"

"Celluloid. It's been known for seventeen years."

Eastman's eyes shone. "Do you know what that means?"

Walker merely nodded.

"You don't know a thing!" blustered Eastman. "Even I can hardly foresee the results."

He obtained the formula for celluloid, which John W. Hyatt, its inventor, had published in 1869, and, with Walker, began to try to adapt this early plastic to his own purpose. Having nitrated cellulose, the purest cotton, in a mixture of sulphuric and nitric acids, they combined it with a solution of camphor in alcohol. The greatest difficulty followed: the solution must be allowed to flow in a thin layer over large plates, and on the evenness and cleanness of those plates would depend the quality of the celluloid sheets. Then they had to wait until the solvent had evaporated—a severe test of Eastman's nerves, but easier for Walker. They had many failures, but one day, at last, Eastman succeeded in stripping from the mirror-smooth plate a celluloid sheet that was hardly a tenth of a millimeter thick.

"A film!" said Walker with a grin. That was his name for the thin skin that formed on heated milk, which he always picked up with two fingers, distastefully, and laid on the saucer.

Film! At the moment he had no idea what significance that word would some day have.

They cut their celluloid film into strips, covered it with gelatin emulsion, rolled it on spools, and put it into Eastman's camera. Everything suddenly seemed so simple—even though celluloid had one disadvantage: it was highly inflammable.

"Now, I think, we can start the triumphal procession!" exclaimed Eastman jubilantly.

Walker had merely a contented smile.

The Eastman Dry Plate and Film Company put its roll film on the market in 1889. Together with the Kodak, which had been introduced the year before, it was a worldwide success. Photography became a popular pastime, and Eastman became a rich man.

"I have reached my goal," declared Eastman to a reporter who had come to interview him, and he squinted over the top of his glasses so that he deepened the two deep creases, running from his nose to his somewhat grim mouth, that reminded one of his poverty-stricken youth. "Or, rather, you will write, of course, that Eastman is happy to have reached his goal: he can offer his customers, for only twenty-five dollars, a Kodak apparatus, enough film for a hundred exposures, and a carrying case. You will also take the opportunity to remind your readers that the equipment required for the same purpose once cost me a hundred dollars. And you may add that for ten dollars the roll of film is developed in my factory, prints are made, a new roll of film is supplied, and the apparatus is sent back by the next mail—as our motto promises!"

"You press the button; we do the rest!" intoned the reporter.

Eastman nodded with satisfaction. "And of course you mustn't forget to mention the reduction of weight. Of the ninety pounds my first outfit weighed, little more than a pound is still there. That's all, I think."

"One more question, King Kodak!" said the reporter. "What does the word 'Kodak' really mean?"

"Nothing at all! I made it up out of thin air. It would be best, of course, for you to write that the word 'Kodak,' philologically, is as meaningless as the babbling of a child. I decided on it simply because it's easy to remember. It is short and convincing, abrupt and rough even to the point of rudeness. Wedged in between the two consonants at the ends, hard as a rock, it hits you in the face like a focal-plane shutter. You can't ask more of a word."

Pleased with himself, Eastman closed the door behind the newspaper man: good publicity is a big part of success. He was about to return to his laboratory when Walker stopped him.

"A gentleman is waiting in the anteroom, a clergyman, who won't be turned away. You will have to see him, Chief, if the place is going to be able to get down to work."

Eastman let himself be persuaded. The clergyman who then entered the room was no longer very young, and he did not look very healthy.

"I am Hannibal Goodwin. Does the name remind you of anything?"

"As far as the 'Hannibal' goes, a partly unpleasant, partly defective memory of my school days, which were too short to leave more behind."

Goodwin did not take up the easy tone. "More than two years ago I applied for an American patent. The patentable idea, Mr. Eastman, was this: strips of celluloid are used to carry a light-sensitive emulsion."

"And what do you mean by that?"

"You have built up a magnificent business here, Mr. Eastman: you make cameras that sell as fast as you can make them; you will become rich and famous. But the solution of the crucial problem—that you owe to me!"

"And so?" The manufacturer waited, on guard.

Goodwin hesitated, as if he were now considering, for the first time, what he had really thought over many times. "How do you intend to preserve my priority, take care of my interests?"

Eastman did not explode, nor did he bluster, as Goodwin had expected; he began, on the contrary, indulgently, as if he were speaking to a child. "Celluloid has been known for a long time and has already been used, I have found, for all sorts of things: dolls, mugs, mirror frames . . . Under these circumstances do you really consider it remarkable to use it also as a base for the photographic emulsion?"

"For your apparatus, nevertheless, it was the decisive invention."

Eastman's eyes became two narrow slits. "Decisive invention! What, Mr. Goodwin, is decisive in photography—optics, the principle of the camera obscura, the sensitivity to light of the silver salts, the method of development, the gelatin, the . . . the . . .? What, Mr. Goodwin, what?"

The clergyman had no answer.

"And here you come and give all the credit to the use of celluloid, a substance that you didn't even invent! Don't you see that here—in technology—a great whole is growing together like the leafy roof of a wide-spreading tree that was only a modest little sapling two centuries ago? Year after year the tree has grown, by limb after limb, by thousands of little branches that weave themselves together. Who on the outside can say from which branch a particular leaf hangs?"

"Very pretty, Mr. Eastman! Some day, perhaps, you can find use for the idea in a schoolbook. Now, however, I am here to claim my prior rights. I shall insist on having them."

The creases in Eastman's face got deeper, got hard. "And where is the patent?" he asked.

"It has not yet been granted."

"Then I will fight it!" The words exploded in the room.

Hannibal Goodwin smiled knowingly. "You are risking a great deal, Mr. Eastman; I risk nothing at all."

Then Eastman lost all his reserve. "Sir, I grew up poor, as poor as a dog, and filled with one idea: that some day I would change that condition. You may believe it or not, but today I still fear poverty as others fear fire. And now you turn up, out of nowhere, and want to climb into the warm nest, want to push me out? What do you expect me to do, sir?" Involuntarily he lowered his head like a bellicose bull. "I'll tell you what you can expect from me: fight and more fight!"

The fight went on for years. The Patent Office finally recognized Goodwin's priority. It did him little good, however, for he died soon afterward in complete poverty.

King Kodak was not disturbed by the decision. In the same year in which Goodwin was granted his patent, 1898, he introduced his folding Kodak, which was much handier than the earlier box-shaped camera. For the photographers of the whole world "Kodak" was a concept, and for the journalists of all the continents Eastman was the perfect example of the self-made man.

He was, besides, a millionaire many times over.

9.

THE SOUND NEEDS PICTURES

THE teacher of ancient history in a little town in Ohio, when he had reached the right point in his course, used to give his pupils an idea of the Greeks' Olympus in the following way: "One day Zeus, father of the gods, decided to assign to each god a certain field of activity: to Poseidon the sea, to Ares commerce and war, to Apollo the fine arts, and so on. He had hardly finished the assignments when an insignificant little god, who felt he had been treated like a stepson, called out, 'And who is to take charge of electricity?' The father of the gods answered him: 'For that appointment I want to wait a few more thousands of years—to be exact, until February 11, 1847, for on that day, in Milan, Ohio, in the future United States of America, a certain Thomas Alva Edison will be born.'" Then the teacher always laughed—more than his pupils, naturally, since he knew the story better than they.

And Edison, in fact, did simply take charge of electricity. He had nothing to do with the investigation of the nature of the new form of energy, for others had taken care of that before him: Guericke first of all, then Galvani, Volta, Oersted, Ampère, Ohm, Faraday, Maxwell, and many others—all resounding names. Edison showed how to produce electricity on a large scale, distribute it, apply it, and make it useful.

It all began, really, with a box on the ear that an excited train conductor gave to young Edison on the line between Port Huron and Detroit. Then, after putting the boy off the train, he threw after him all his belongings—and not without justification, for they had set fire to a car.

Tom sat on the embankment among his damaged possessions and cursed the wretched track, which had shaken up his chemicals so badly that a piece of phosphorus had caught fire. Then he felt sorry that his good job was finished. When he was twelve years old, he had begun to sell newspapers in the train in order to increase his pocket money by enough to pay for books and to satisfy his insatiable desire to experiment. He had really earned enough only after he began to print, on the moving train, his own little paper, reporting the most important local news, and to sell it as a supplement to the Detroit papers.

All that was over now, and at first the only thing that seemed to matter was the piercing pain in his ear. The angry conductor had really slapped him hard, and for a time Tom could hear nothing.

What sort of work should he take up now? This question seemed to have only one answer. Selling papers didn't really bring in enough money to pay for experiments, and he knew he couldn't compete with trained typesetters. His recently acquired skill in telegraphy and his knowledge of electricity were all he had to brag about. Not long before, he had saved the life of a child of a stationmaster on the railway line, and the grateful father had taught him how to use Morse's telegraph, which was spreading quickly over the country and had become indispensable to the railroads. Telegraphy, though still young, was the only application that really put electricity to full use; it could employ a capable fellow who really understood it.

For five years Edison wandered through the states and Canada, working as a telegrapher.

Then he had had enough. He had, it is true, earned a living, but he had not been able to save for the new experiments. How, without money, could he find out all the things that electricity could do? He told himself that he must approach the problem in some other way, and in 1869, looking for an opportunity, he arrived in New York with just one dollar in his pocket.

The opportunity presented itself immediately. Entering the dispatching office of a firm that operated a telegraphic service reporting stock-market prices to brokers, Edison found himself in a crowd of excited messenger boys from the brokers' offices. The telegraphic dispatching instrument had broken down, and the frantic brokers had sent their messengers for news of the market. Edison offered to repair the instrument, saw at once what had caused the breakdown, and soon had the reports flying along the wires to the brokers' offices. The reporting firm, Western Union, hired him at once, at a good salary, to supervise the operation of its equipment. During the same year, having patented an improvement on the price-quoting telegraph, now known as the ticker, Edison sold his device to his employer for $40,000.

Now things were going as they should! The sum was a small fortune in those days, and many men would have retired on it; but Edison couldn't get rid of it fast enough. Undertaking new experiments with electricity, he set up his first laboratory in Newark (New Jersey). He was soon granted sixty-nine different patents in telegraphy. Among his employees were Europeans who, when they returned home a little later, became pioneers of electrotechnology in their own countries.

Two of Edison's closest collaborators, John Kruesi and Charles Batchelor, used to argue about his motives, Kruesi maintaining that only electricity aroused his deep interest, Batchelor often finding other reasons for what he did. Edison seemed to confirm Kruesi when, one day, beaming with good humor, he sat down between them to talk. He had married Mary Stilwell, eight years younger than himself, and all the happiness of new marriage glowed in his youthful eyes. "The only things she carries on about," he remarked, "are my black coffee and my thick cigars. They are bad for me, she says. I have explained to her that people who work with great concentration often resort to such aids. But my health seems to mean more to her than the progress of electrotechnology. Do you agree with her?"

With his irrepressible young man's laugh he took out a fresh cigar, lit it, and blew the smoke comfortably toward the ceiling.

"I really wanted to talk to you about something else. Does either of you know Menlo Park?"

The mechanics shook their heads.

"I'm not surprised," said Edison. "It's only a little place— no more than seven houses. But take note of the name, for we are moving there. The surroundings are so beautiful and healthful that I want my wife—and later my children—to enjoy them."

His collaborators merely nodded; they had expected something of the sort.

"And there's where we shall really dig into electricity!" Edison's eyes shone with the strange light that they knew well. "The telegraph is very good, but what small currents it uses! I know, someone is supposed to be working on a device that will carry the voice from place to place by wire, but that too will use only small currents. Is that the end of electrotechnology? With such a magnificent form of energy one must be able to do much greater things. And that's our job!"

Kruesi gave Batchelor a triumphant, challenging look, as if to say, "Well, isn't this just what I was saying?" Batchelor could only answer with a lifeless grin.

All this was reason for Kruesi to be astonished at one of

the first tasks assigned to him after the move to Menlo Park (New Jersey) in 1876. Edison had given him a rough sketch on which was scrawled (Edison could still not spell Kruesi's name): "Kreusi make this." What could this be? There was a cylinder with a fine spiral groove and a crank for turning it! And a needle, which apparently was meant to follow the groove, was set in the middle of a membrane at the base of a cone! That was all; there were no electrical connections, no switch, no magnet!

"Well, what's that funny thing got to do with electricity?" asked Batchelor exultantly, and this time Kruesi had no answer.

When the thing was finished and stood ready on the bench, Edison called together several of his closest collaborators, including Kruesi and Batchelor. As they watched, he carefully applied to the cylinder a sheet of tin foil. Then, as he turned the cylinder with the crank, he recited into the cone an old nursery rhyme, "Mary had a little lamb." The membrane, set into motion by his voice, impressed its vibrations, through the needle, on the tin foil that covered the passing grooves of the cylinder. The impressions were deep enough to set the membrane in vibration again when Edison silently repeated the operation. "Mary had a little lamb . . .," said the cone.

"Mein Gott im Himmel!" exclaimed Kruesi, lapsing into his native German.

"A machine that talks!" stammered Batchelor, as if he had seen a miracle.

Kruesi was the first to come to himself. "How did you ever hit on that, Chief?"

"By accident." The inventor, happy and satisfied, smiled broadly. "I was really working on a sort of automatic telegraph, in which a second needle, running through the impressions made by the first, would pick them up and send them out over the wires as electric impulses. While I was thinking about it, I remembered an old toy, a little figure cut out of paper, which the air vibrations of the human voice set into motion. Shouldn't it be possible, I asked myself, to impress these vibrations, as well as the Morse signals, on a surface?"

He let the needle run through the groove again, and again they heard the cone saying, "Mary had a little lamb . . ." And, even though it sounded simple as Edison had explained it, they remained astonished.

The rest of the world was even more astonished. A fine demonstration of that took place in Paris, at the Academy of Sciences. When a well-known physicist demonstrated a talking machine there for the first time, one of his colleagues fell on him in a rage, seized him by the throat, and cried: "You scoundrel! Do you really think we are going to let ourselves be taken in by a ventriloquist?"

People were soon talking about the "magician of Menlo Park," as A. E. Beach, the editor of the *Scientific American*, had named Edison. "If the idea of an 'accidental invention' is ever justified," he wrote, "the Phonograph, Edison's talking machine, certainly deserves to be so called. Not because Edison succeeded in reproducing the human voice more or less casually, you might say, and at the first attempt. No, it's not for that reason at all, but because nobody had even dreamed of this possibility. Ordinarily problems go flickering through the world, like will-o'-the-wisps, for decades before someone succeeds in solving them. But who had ever thought of recording the human voice? No one, as the Patent Office admits. When, on February 19, 1878, hardly fifty days after the application, the Office granted Edison the memorable patent No. 200,521, it pointed out that the invention was unique: according to its records, no one had ever before tried to reproduce the human voice mechanically."

If Edison did not want to disappoint either Zeus or the history teacher in Ohio, he would now have to put aside the Phonograph, which did, in fact, have nothing to do—at that time—with electricity. And that is what he did for a time—regretfully, for the Phonograph remained his favorite.

"It's the same with him, Batch, as with many fathers," said Kruesi. "When, of all his splendid children, one is noticeable for some peculiarity, his special love goes out to that one."

"Sometimes I believe you would have made a quite passable philosopher," answered Batchelor.

"Even a complete blockhead could see that the man must always come back to electricity. What I regret is that fate had to team me up with you, of all people!"

Edison came back to electricity by inventing the carbon microphone and thus perfecting the telephone recently patented by Alexander Graham Bell.

"Do you know why the Chief improved the telephone?" asked Batchelor.

Kruesi found the question so silly that he didn't bother to answer it.

"It's because he hears so badly since that train conductor boxed his ears."

Kruesi scratched under his cap before he answered. "I don't agree with you, Batch. The Chief will take on anything that has anything to do with electricity."

"That's one explanation," admitted Batchelor. "Maybe it's better than mine, but mine is more natural."

Having acquired fresh capital by selling the microphone to Western Union for $100,000, Edison took up a new task—the creation of an incandescent lamp. The problem was an old one. Innumerable clever heads had been trying for decades to find a way of illuminating by means of fine wires that were made to glow by electric current. Twenty-five years earlier a German, Heinrich Goebel, had perhaps come the closest to solving this problem. Many were said to have become discouraged recently when some well-known English scientists had again declared the problem to be insoluble.

Edison was not discouraged.

With his unique concentration and the doggedness of one who feels that he has a mission, he tackled the problem. He began long series of experiments. The fine wires that he fused into glass bulbs burned up, even those made out of the most unusual materials. If they were not to burn up, he must pump the oxygen out of the bulbs. In order to do that, however, he must first improve the air pump. Then followed new experiments—hundreds of them, thousands. For more than a year Edison struggled with the problem of the incandescent lamp. He thought of nothing else. Those around him thought his concentration was absent-mindedness.

He finally gave up the experiments with metallic filaments and went back to the carbon filament that had burned up quickly in the air-filled bulb. And in a vacuum the carbon filament held: six hours, ten hours . . . For all participants, including Edison, it was exciting, after the months of disappointment, of sometimes pretended confidence, simply to see the lamp burning . . . thirty, forty, forty-five hours.

That was on October 21, 1879. New, apparently endless series of experiments were needed now to find the best carbon fiber, one that would last for two hundred or, even better, fifteen hundred hours. A bamboo fiber finally turned out to be the best.

By that time the greatness of his task had taken possession of Edison. He rushed, as he admitted later, into the "greatest adventure" of his life. The technically new territory he was entering seemed to stretch away without end. The new light bulbs had to be provided with sockets, with switches, with fuses, in every house, in every room; had to be served with underground cables, with parts for making connections, with meters; and to all this must be added power plants with dynamos and innumerable accessories. Nothing of the sort existed, nothing even similar—no models that he could follow.

All that was electrical engineering; that was Edison's mission.

On September 4, 1882, on Pearl Street in New York, the first big electric power plant in the world was put into operation.

But Pearl Street was only a modest beginning.

In 1887 Edison moved his laboratory to West Orange (New Jersey), and soon afterward he agreed to take a short vacation—on the urging of his wife, who had in mind a week or so of relaxation at the seaside or in the mountains, or of simple rest in the magnificent garden at Menlo Park.

On the first day he let himself be persuaded to take a long walk, and he himself even planned a trip to the mountains. In the evening, when they were sitting at ease in the living room, he brought out his Phonograph. "It's my favorite, as they all say," said Edison gaily, "and I can't imagine an hour of recreation without it." He cranked the cylinder through its recording. The second time he found the cranking to be a nuisance. The third time he decided that the cylinder must certainly be turned by a motor.

On the second day he built a motor drive for the Phonograph; the rest of the day was enough for a march round Menlo Park. In the evening he decided that it was a bore to listen to the same cylinder all the time. The cylinder must be changeable, so that one could record different pieces of music, even long ones. His wife glanced mistrustfully at him.

In the following days he changed the apparatus. But every day he saved an hour for strolling with his wife through the park.

And then a new idea invaded the restless Edison's mind. "One really ought to build an apparatus that would do for the eye what the talking machine does for the ear—a complement to the Phonograph, you might say."

His wife slowly raised her head. A deep, suspicious wrinkle stood between her eyebrows.

"They cannot, of course, be pictures as boring as a glance into one's familiar living room. They must bring change, must show the course of some fascinating action, must pass the time while one is listening to the Phonograph."

"You remind me," said his wife, trying to pass his idea off as a joke, "of a father who is determined to rig up some comical toy for his favorite child."

"And that you understand!"

With those words he disappeared. The laboratory had swallowed him up, him and those fine vacation plans.

He had remembered a series of pictures that he had once seen in the *Scientific American*. Groping his way, he came upon all the serial photographs, and he was surprised to find how many besides Muybridge had been busy with them: the Frenchmen Marey and Duboscq; the Viennese Theodor Reich, who lived in London; Le Prince; Friese-Greene . . . A seemingly endless chain of names was written down in his already famous notebooks. Ottomar Anschütz fascinated him more than any of the others, less by the amazing quality of his pictures than by his apparatus for looking at them, which came the closest to what Edison had—still vaguely—in mind. Watching in Anschütz's Rapid Viewer the quick passage of twenty-four transparencies divided between two disks, which alternately stood still for a fraction of a second, the observer had the illusion of seeing—for one example—a flying bird.

While he was investigating serial photographs, Edison discovered that his collaborators, despite all his precautions, had looted his stock of cigars to a degree that called for punishment. Oh, what rogues! His method of revenge corresponded to his youthful nature. The next morning he ordered from his dealer a few boxes of specially rolled cigars, filled with sawdust and tea leaves. He carried them to the laboratory soon afterward with a mischievous grin; the dealer had assured him that they would produce the most repulsive smoke that a man had ever drawn into his lungs.

During the evening of that day Edison came to the conclusion that Anschütz's Rapid Viewer was not what the

Phonograph needed. The conclusion cost an imposing number of cigars. His wife complained when she counted the butts, no doubt with reason. But Edison only smiled. What was bad for him had aided his reflections, he thought, and he had decided that his child, the Phonograph, needed to be accompanied by longer, more exciting scenes—little theatrical scenes, which, if possible, should run as long as the sound recordings. He must combine single pictures into long strips, and for that purpose glass would not do. He needed a transparent material, light and flexible, that could be formed into long strips.

There would be no difficulty in finding such a material. For what other purpose did he have his collection of all known raw materials, of which he was so proud that he had promised to pay a dollar to anyone who failed to find such a material in it? There he found George Eastman's Kodak film.

He wrote to Rochester.

For $2.50 he got a strip of celluloid fifty feet long. On this he intended to mount his carefully exposed serial pictures. But he smoked many cigars before he had decided how to divide up the strip. A fortunate choice of dimensions has always been a decisive factor in the world of technology. Edison decided to make each little picture twenty-four millimeters (about four-fifths of an inch) wide and eighteen millimeters (about three-fifths of an inch) high. Rollers with little cogs would engage the strip through little holes punched at regular intervals along both sides. A width of thirty-five millimeters for the whole strip seemed to him to allow space enough for the punched holes. And how close together should the holes be? That too was an important decision and required a cigar. He decided to put four holes on each side of each picture. (See the diagram on page 235.)

Edison had no idea, at the time, how firmly, by these decisions, he was impressing the stamp of his personality on the world.

The apparatus itself, compared with the other problems, offered no difficulties. The endless strip of mounted pictures must simply be carried over a series of rollers, which would be turned with a crank. Or should he provide a motor right away? Perhaps it was more important, at first, to build the whole apparatus into a case so that the observer could easily approach the window. A moving shutter would have to be mounted behind the window to conceal the change of pictures, but that was a simple job for Kruesi and Batchelor. It was too bad, of course, that only one person at a time could look at the flitting pictures.

Satisfied, Edison reached for another cigar. He noticed that his supply was getting low. Besides, he told himself, that careless dealer should have delivered the cigars for his practical joke long before this! He complained the next day. The dealer looked at him with unmistakable pity. "You took them away with you," he said. "I guess you must have smoked those cigars yourself."

Edison, thoroughly confused, tried to explain his absent-mindedness: "I've been very busy lately."

"It certainly must have been with something very special, Mr. Edison!"

"Perhaps it would be better," answered Edison meekly, "if from now on you simply delivered your best kind again."

Kruesi and Batchelor built the Kinetoscope, as Edison had named his new apparatus.

"It's a fine peep-show," exulted Kruesi, "and at last something new that will be fun for everybody!"

Batchelor shifted his chewing gum from the left side to the right, then from the right to the left—something he always did when he was about to deliver what he considered an important explanation. "Your observations are good, John, but not exhaustive; for, as a matter of fact, everything the Chief has brought out gives pleasure to everybody: the improved telephone, the Phonograph, the incandescent lamp.

Or don't you think so? Look, here is why everybody likes him. Earlier"—his gesture pointed at least a hundred years back—"people invented all sorts of things. But who gets pleasure out of a steam engine that puffs away inside a mine, out of a mechanical loom that rattles away in a textile factory? The owners, industry! His things, on the contrary, make life pleasanter for everybody. It will be the same with that thing." He paused. "I don't know whether you really understand me."

"Look here, you're not so frightfully subtle as all that!" exclaimed Kruesi.

"And there's another point to remember, John!" Batchelor rolled his gum around again. "If the whole much-touted technological evolution is to make any sense, the machines must take more and more work away from us people. And what will be the result? That there is more and more leisure— for everybody. And what does that mean? Well?"

Kruesi did not answer. He was busy, at the moment, trying to stretch a long strip of film through the intricate system of rollers by which the observer would crank more than a thousand separate little pictures past the viewing window. The layman may think that this was no world-shaking task, but it demanded a mechanic of great skill. How many people remember, Kruesi was thinking, that the realization of even great ideas depends on the adroitness of two hands?

"It looks as if that thick Swiss skull of yours had not entirely followed my magnificent thoughts, John. But, since I am your friend, I shall throw light on the business again, and from another side. In the future, it's admitted, people will have more free time at their disposal. And what will they need then? Amusement, and still more amusement! Can you imagine anything better adapted to that purpose than the Phonograph and the Kinetoscope? I tell you that this box will be worth more than everything the Chief has produced up to now. I just hope that he realizes this and puts all his energy into the Kinetoscope."

Since Kruesi responded with too little enthusiasm, Batchelor expressed the same idea to Edison—with somewhat more moderation, to be sure. The inventor declared that he had something more important to do at the moment and cut Batchelor short with a cigar.

Edison exhibited both pieces of apparatus together—the Phonograph and the Kinetoscope—to the editor-in-chief of the New York *Herald*. He called the combination his Kinetophone.

The newspaperman looked dubiously over the top of his glasses. "You couldn't think of a more pompous name, Mr. Edison? Or have you forgotten that complicated ideas have never yet become popular?"

But he grinned when one of Edison's collaborators appeared in the window of the apparatus, bowed, and asked in a croaking membrane voice: "What do you have to say about the Kinetophone, Mr. Edison?"

The inventor had a second scene run off: Batchelor appeared in the window and loudly and clearly counted his fingers, pointing to each. With this film Edison wanted to demonstrate clearly the synchronization between picture and sound—the problem that bothered him the most.

The editor was, of course, astonished by the technical achievement and admired the novelty of the idea, but Edison missed the enthusiasm that he was already used to hearing. Certainly, he thought, the synchronization was not satisfactory.

That had been on October 6, 1889.

Since then Edison had—in Batchelor's mind, at least—neglected the Kinetoscope inexcusably. Batchelor, still firmly convinced of the Kinetoscope's importance, brought the subject up again. But Edison, captivated by a new series of experiments (he wanted to create a storage battery that would be more efficient and more rugged than the lead battery), disappointed him. "I have made my contribution, the technical development, with the Kinetoscope," he said. "In the future the important question will be what the apparatus shows, how the films are put together. That's a job for other hands. I hope they do it well, for when I consider how easily people are influenced by what they see, I must regard the Kinetoscope as one of the most powerful instruments on earth."

Batchelor scratched his stubbly chin. What was an honest mechanic to make of such phrases? He returned to Kruesi in a bad humor.

"John, I sometimes believe the Chief is spoiled. If they don't send him the patent by return mail, as they did for the Phonograph, he loses interest. Because they have called his attention to the English apparatus, the one made by that fellow Friese-Greene, he doesn't want to hear any more about the Kinetoscope."

"It's not that," growled Kruesi.

"I insist, too, that there's a real difference between them. Sure, Friese-Greene also uses a strip of celluloid. But how does he move it along? With a sort of bat! Just imagine, John, a circling peg, which knocks the film along—isn't that asking for trouble? It can't stand comparison with our punched holes. And the Chief wants to shove a thing like that calmly to one side! Thousands of inventors—those with the patented miracle hairbrushes and the patented combinations of toothpicks and shoehorns—would be overjoyed to have such an idea! But what does he do with it? Nothing! He has made his contribution, he says. If that isn't a crime!" He filed fanatically at a steel cell for the new storage battery, laid the square against it, held it up against the light, and continued to file.

"Perhaps," Batchelor began again after a while, "he's upset because the pictures and the sound are not perfectly synchronized. But who says that everything depends on that?"

"It's not that," repeated Kruesi.

"It's not that!" repeated Batchelor. "That's just what I've been saying. It's much more important, for example, to arrange things so that more than one person can look at the pictures, isn't it? Well, then, he must keep after it! Eighty more patents have already been added to the original patent on the Phonograph! In any case he can't just let the thing slide, leave it to other hands, as he says, if he believes it will become the most powerful instrument on earth!"

"You'll never learn, Batch," said Kruesi. Then he edged up close to his friend and spoke softly, as if he were confiding a secret: "Haven't I always told you that none of us should be messing around with pictures and sound? The Chief least of all! That's why he doesn't want to hear any more about that gadget. He belongs, body and soul, to electricity!"

10.

SEE YOURSELF AS OTHERS SEE YOU

COURTESY and glibness were elements of Monsieur Carnot's charm. His work, indeed, as manager of the Grand Café on the Boulevard des Capucines, in Paris, required those qualities—and elegance too.

"Gentlemen, I am desolated!" he groaned. "But with that price I have reached the limit of my extraordinary generosity. I therefore permit myself to repeat: thirty francs a day, the rent for a year to be paid in advance."

The two gentlemen facing him betrayed by their appearance that they came from the provinces and by their resemblance that they were brothers. Both had tangled, curly black hair, retreating at the corners of the forehead, and under their aggressive noses drooped ungroomed bushy mustaches. One of them wore a pince-nez, apparently for no other reason than to distinguish himself from his brother.

They exchanged looks before the one with the merrily sparkling eyes, who sat at the window, began, obviously distressed, to speak somewhat haltingly. "That is terrible, Monsieur Carnot—almost discouraging! You probably don't realize that the public performance of our Cinematograph will be a sensation, a unique, perhaps a historical, event, which is worthy of every consideration. Who has ever shown such moving pictures?"

"Oh, take care, sir!" Unmistakable compassion stole into Carnot's smile. "Emile Reynaud is showing moving pictures— not far from here, in his Optical Theater. A certain Le Prince—perhaps the name is known to you—is said to have constructed an apparatus for the same purpose. The man has disappeared without a trace, to be sure, on a trip to Dijon; so he no longer counts. But there are two men from Berlin— they also happen to be brothers—who were recently looking for an exhibition room here; for French tongues their name is hardly pronounceable: Skla-da-now-sky!"

The brother wearing the glasses, with a gesture of dismissal, spoke up. "Sir, Max and Emil Skladanowsky use a double projector. Their method can't stand comparison with ours. Two strips of film, each with its ends pasted together to form a loop, are projected alternately on the screen. How complicated!"

"And what do they offer?" the other brother interjected. "One scene eternally repeating itself! The usual club-swingers and jumpers and a friendly gentleman tipping his hat!"

The brother with the glasses again intervened. "And how are the strips moved along? With metal eyelets in the perforations! With metal eyelets, Monsieur Carnot!"

"Whether it's a double projector or not—that's too much for my understanding. Whether eyelets or not—that doesn't interest me. I have found out, however, that the brothers exhibited their Bioscope last November in Berlin, in the Winter Garden variety theater, and with dazzling success. It's even said that the newspapers reported the event!"

"Why?" Now the brother at the window, with a sudden burst of southern temperament, was getting excited. "Why, Monsieur Carnot? Because people everywhere are demanding a solution of this problem! For years, for decades, they have been demanding moving pictures. Life, movement! Just con-

sider the magic power exerted by movement! Have you ever
sat at the edge of a brook, or by a river, bewitched by the
play of the waves? Could you tear yourself away?"

"With all respect for your enthusiasm, sir, I ask: Who
guarantees that *you* will fulfill this dream?"

The man with the glasses advanced again in his deliberate
way. "We have, after all, received a French patent." He
reached into his pocket, unfolded a document, and began to
read: "Patent No. 245,032, of February 13, 1895, to Louis
and Auguste Lumière: Apparatus for obtaining and exhibiting chronophotographic exposures. Distinguishing characteristics: The picture-carrier, a strip perforated at regular intervals, is moved along in jerks by a mechanism, a system of
claws, during dark periods brought about by a shutter. The
movement of the strip is interrupted at regular intervals, during which the pictures appear on the screen."

"For heaven's sake, sir," groaned Carnot, "you are certainly not going to spoil the pleasure of your visit by asking
me to listen to the full text of an official document!"

The more adroit of the two brothers intervened. "We
exhibited our apparatus about a year ago to the Society for
the Promotion of National Industry. Berthelot was there,
wasn't he, Louis?" The other's glasses blinked agreement.
"And he was enthusiastic—simply enchanted!"

"Then you will certainly be successful here too, gentlemen, with your public performances, and you will have no
trouble in paying the thirty francs a day."

Auguste Lumière, embarrassed, scratched behind his ear,
his eyes narrow slits. "That's not the point. Inventors must,
by their very nature, be confident. What embarrasses us—
for the moment—is simply your demand that we pay the
rent for a year in advance. Where would we get so much
money now?"

"But in Lyon," said Carnot in astonishment, "you own a
factory producing photographic plates and chemicals. In view

of the current interest in photography, that must be a dazzling success."

"That may be, but in recent years we have had tremendous expenses. We have had to buy apparatus after apparatus—every type we could find. And why? In order to learn, always to learn, to discover the advantages of every type. Only then did our work begin: a new apparatus, built according to our ideas. That costs money, Monsieur Carnot, a great deal of money. The optical components alone! We had them made by Jules Carpentier, of course—no doubt a master in his field, but expensive, very expensive!" The corners of his mouth appeared from under his mustache and sank resignedly to his chin. "For half a year we devoted ourselves to this task alone, day after day and night after night. You will realize that our manufacturing business suffered. We were fascinated by our idea."

"That may well be, but . . ."

Auguste interrupted the manager. "Don't misunderstand us. We don't object to the amount of the rent; we are simply troubled by the difficulty of paying a full year's rent in advance. We therefore ask you again to consider our offer: twenty percent of the proceeds, payable daily."

"Twenty percent, gentlemen! How enticing if you only half fill the hall! But who guarantees even that?"

"You have little confidence . . ."

"And much experience," answered Carnot promptly.

An oppressive silence settled over the room. All three sighed with relief when the light ticking of the clock was drowned by the striking of the hour. Three pairs of eyes turned at the same time to the mantelpiece. Just above the clock hung an old daguerreotype—presumably a picture of the last owner of the Grand Café.

Monsieur Carnot, clearing his throat, said: "In order to prove to you that I am as enthusiastic about photography as every Frenchman should be, I submit to you my final proposal. You should be able to begin your performances before New Year's Day. If they come up to your expectations, you will certainly be able to find a financial backer within three days, and it will be easy for you to pay the rent on January 1." He smiled maliciously.

"You are very cunning, Monsieur Carnot."

"Let us not waste our precious time on compliments," said the manager, reaching for pen and ink. "May I write out the lease?"

"Must it be in writing?"

"For the sake of security."

The two brothers looked at each other dubiously.

"Thirty times 365 makes almost 11,000 francs," said Louis with a sigh. "That's a great deal for a room that hardly holds more than a hundred persons—a hundred and twenty at the most—and is really nothing but a vaulted cellar."

"Pardon me, sir!" Carnot became stony. "You are forgetting the unique location. And if the hall—admittedly—is a little below the street level, where, I ask, would you find a room exposed to full sunlight that could be completely darkened? And that's an important point with you, isn't it?"

"Twenty percent—payable daily," the brother at the window reminded him.

"I am inconsolable," said Carnot, shrugging and beginning to put away his writing gear.

The two brothers nodded together as if on order; they gave up.

"I rejoice that we could reach an agreement so quickly," said the manager of the Grand Café triumphantly, setting pen to paper with a flourish. "What did you say your name was?"

"Lumière."

"And your dates of birth?"

"Born in Besançon: Auguste in 1862, Louis in 1864."

On December 28, 1895, life surged back and forth on the

Boulevard des Capucines very much as on any other day—
except that the exhilaration of the holiday season had brought
out an unusual number of strollers. But very few stopped at
the Grand Café before the sign that promised them twenty
sensational minutes for one franc: the first public exhibition
of the cinematographic pictures of the Lumière brothers.

A franc was a good deal of money. Most of the strollers
were kept out by the entrance fee, and only a few felt their
way down the dimly lighted steps into the basement hall.

Louis Lumière stepped out in front of the screen, which
was stretched tight without a wrinkle, and began to speak in
an embarrassed manner. He and his brother, Auguste, he said,
had become acquainted with Edison's Kinetoscope on an
earlier trip to Paris. The magic of moving pictures had over-
powered them, taken them captive. Beginning with Stampfer's Stroboscope, they had followed Uchatius's brilliant
train of thought, and had studied—thoroughly studied—
Marey's photographic rifle and Anschütz's Rapid Viewer—as
well as the excellent apparatus of a Viennese living in London, a certain Theodor Reich. Only after such studies had
they set about creating something new. They had, of course,
retained the valuable, usable elements of the other devices—
for example, Edison's dimensions for the strip of film. In
conclusion Louis Lumière mentioned the solemnity of the
present moment, in which they would see the realization of
one of humanity's ancient dreams—one that would, perhaps,
herald a new age.

In the yawning emptiness of the hall his words sounded
too theatrical.

Then it became dark. The projector began to rattle. On
the screen appeared workmen, leaving the Lumière brothers'
factory in Lyon, in groups, talking, laughing. Jolly faces
dispensed the quitting-time mood that the cameraman,
standing opposite the factory, must have felt. Among the
workmen a boy, who had stared too long at the camera,
stumbled on the curbstone. After one or two minutes the

scene changed. "Blacksmiths at work," Louis announced, trying to make himself heard above the noise of the projector. This strip of film, like the one before, ran from the projector into a laundry basket lying on the floor. Beside the basket, smoking cigars, sat spectators, none of whom had any idea that the film was dangerously inflammable. The "Life on Exchange Place in Lyon" seemed to be taking place in the rain. But the spectators had already got used to the fine lines, scratched in the sensitive emulsion by the apparatus, that ran up and down the picture. The last scene won the greatest applause: A gardener got himself so horribly entangled in his hose that the full force of the stream of water hit him right in the face.

The incandescent lights on the ceiling came on. Auguste wound the strips of film back on their spools for the next performance, and the spectators, carefully climbing the steps, argued whether they had seen eight films or ten.

At the top of the steps stood Monsieur Carnot. He counted carefully. By evening he had counted thirty-five spectators. Was that enough to persuade a financier to back the brothers? All he needed to know—and he was an excellent calculator—was that twenty percent of thirty-five francs was seven francs. Enough! It would have been foolish, irresponsible, to let himself be taken in by the two brothers. This was no sensation! With a self-satisfied gesture he smoothed down his perfectly fitting waistcoat.

As the last spectators passed him, one of them, a stout man, was saying to his younger companion: "Did you notice how small the attendance was, Mr. Gibson? Fatal, simply fatal!"

The two were already strolling down the Boulevard des Capucines when the stout one resumed his train of thought: "I sometimes wonder if the Lumière brothers were not imprudent when they plunged into this cinematography, as they call it. Why did they need to do it? They were producing first-class photographs in color by Lippmann's interference method. Louis—by far the better head, incidentally—showed me a picture himself: A table stands in front of a green wall of grape leaves. Fruit and a bottle of red wine are on the table, and between them, on the table top, a girl is sleeping. She had to be asleep, of course, for otherwise she could not have endured the long exposure. That was the first color photograph that reproduced correctly the color shading of the human skin! And that technique, which could have been developed, they both abandoned when Edison's Kinetoscope bewitched them!"

The younger man walked on a little before speaking. "It seems to me, Monsieur Carpentier, that the pictures are amazingly quiet on the screen—at least quieter than those of LeRoy, which I saw in New York. Two years ago, working toward the same goal, LeRoy exhibited his art in an optician's shop, probably with a similar apparatus. But one question remains in my mind: In what way have the Lumières made an advance?"

"I can answer that question for you: in the simplicity, my young friend, in the amazing simplicity of the apparatus. During my collaboration with the brothers I saw enough to enable me to make that judgment. It's an old law of engineering that the simplest apparatus is also the best. I don't mean that the Lumières' procedure does not need improvement. The film transport is not exact enough, and it damages the film, for the claws, after repeated performances, put too great a strain on the soft celluloid; and the laundry basket, with its inflammable contents, is, frankly, a menace —the reason why I insisted on sitting near the door. But all those problems can be solved. The two brothers have accomplished the main task."

"Perhaps—speaking a foreign language—I have not expressed myself clearly enough, Monsieur Carpentier. The brothers admit themselves that they have adopted structural parts from others, and they boast of having retained Edison's dimensions for the film. They are even said to have borrowed the name Cinematograph from someone else. What have they given us that's new?"

"I grant, Mr. Gibson, that they have not contributed any essentially new element. Why? Because there was no need for them to! Weren't all the necessary elements lying ready in the world of applied science, waiting to be picked up and used? They have been ready for years, some of them for decades! Weren't they, in a sense, simply waiting to be fitted together into a great whole? And now I ask you: Is it not a great technical feat to have taken that decisive step?"

The young American did not know what to answer.

"We must not forget, however, that there are always two questions to ask about such ventures. First: Is the time—or, more exactly, technique—ripe for the combination? That question is what defeated, among others, Uchatius, the ingenious Austrian, who, half a century ago, had no instantaneous photography, no celluloid, no electric light. Second: Is society ready for the innovation?"

"What do you mean by that?"

"Perhaps a comparison will be helpful. What would the invention of printing have meant to a world of illiterates, to a society in which most people could never acquire the basis of all education—the ability to read?"

The other answered with a smile. "And, as applied to cinematography . . .?"

"This art may, no doubt, open the way to a pleasanter form of leisure. But of what use can it be to people who have no leisure, who, to earn their living, have to toil every day until they are exhausted?"

"And how do you answer the two questions?"

"The first question, whether technique is ripe, we can answer with a loud 'yes'. The second, whether society is ready—well, we shall have to wait to see what happens."

After a while Gibson said: "When I listen to you, Monsieur Carpentier, I wonder if you are really an optician. You sound more like a philosopher."

"That is simply the heritage of old Europe! You Americans—in the free land of work—have been born into the world of applied science; you take it more casually, more realistically, than we do. We have watched it grow, and we like to philosophize about it."

In the dark basement, in the pale light of a dirty bulb, the Lumière brothers examined the contents of the tin cash-box. Auguste emptied it onto the smooth table top and put thirty francs to one side. With a doleful face he stared at the five remaining coins, and Louis did the same.

Auguste slept badly that night. When, for the eighth time, he had started up out of an oppressive dream, he found that he had been awakened by a coachman, who, on the other side of the street, was trying, without sparing his voice, to persuade some nocturnal revelers to take a ride in his hack. We must go after customers with the same energy, thought Auguste—but in a more subtle way. He turned from one side to the other; after every tenth breath he changed his position. Suddenly he had an idea that seemed, among the confused images of the sleepless night, to be promising. He then fell asleep, confident and at ease.

The next day the bustle on the Boulevard des Capucines was enriched by something new: at the most congested spot a stocky man had set up a heavy tripod, which supported an unwieldy box. Although the box looked amazingly like a camera, the man, strange to say, now and then turned a crank on it. Between cranks Auguste addressed the passerby: "Ladies and gentlemen! You have just been cinematically photographed. If you want to be astonished by seeing yourself, come tomorrow to the Grand Café, to the unique exhibitions of the Lumière brothers. Entrance fee: only one franc." Then he cranked again.

And they came—even the top-hatted gentlemen and the ladies wearing whipping ostrich feathers on their hats, which, as big as wagon wheels, had interfered frightfully with their visibility. They rejoiced at themselves, waved to themselves, saw, with astonishment, their own mannerisms. And—the most important point—they told their acquaintances about this extraordinary encounter and thus, in the best possible way, promoted the business of the Lumière brothers.

They came, the curious ones, by dozens, by hundreds, by thousands and still more thousands. It looked as if everyone who left the hall smiling with satisfaction had nothing more pressing to do than to collect a swarm of friends and relatives and come back with them.

The congestion in front of the Grand Café increased from day to day. The police had to intervene to preserve order. The visitors crowded in more and more excitedly, though Auguste and his assistant now only pretended to take pictures as they cranked the odd-looking box on the Boulevard des Capucines. They had stopped putting film into the box; that was no longer necessary. The people came streaming in anyway. An incomprehensible magic power seemed to be exerted by these films, a relentless power that took possession of all who saw them.

The brothers had easily found a financial backer.

Monsieur Carnot stood hidden by the drapes of his window in the second story, just over the entrance to what was, at that moment, the most famous basement in the world. Recently a sign had been put up there: Lumière Cinematograph. So it *was* a sensation!

He looked enviously at the tumult. Yesterday he had counted two thousand five hundred visitors. Two thousand five hundred! How many would there be today?

He was still good at figures: twenty percent of two thousand five hundred francs was five hundred francs. And he was a fool.

Whenever his circling thoughts came back to this realization, he turned green and yellow, and his face lost the amiable expression that people had always found so pleasing.

11.

A DECISIVE INVENTION

"I HAVE produced forty thousand microscopes and sold them in all parts of the world. That's enough for me." Eduard Messter gestured as if he were totaling up his life. "Now it's your turn, Oskar."

Oskar Messter, in 1892, was twenty-six years old. Although he had known for a long time that this day was bound to come, a wonderful feeling came over him now that it was here. A strange tingling crept clear out to the ends of his fingers. He looked at his mother, who was wiping her cheeks with the corner of her apron. Such solemn occasions always cost her a few tears.

"You understand, of course," continued his father, "that you take over, along with the shop, the obligation to support your parents, by a suitable annuity, during the evening of their lives—and regardless of the course of business, Oskar!"

Even the mother was shocked by the size of the annuity he mentioned.

"Let it stand, Marie!" said the old mechanic defensively. "If he takes proper care of the shop, he'll be able to pay it all right. How, after all, did I begin? With nothing, with nothing at all! I was nineteen years old when I left Siemens & Halske because I wanted, at any price, to be on my own. And at last I was even able to put in steam power to drive my lens-grinders!"

"And that's when you went bankrupt, too, Eduard."

"Right!" Father Messter, embarrassed, scratched his gray temples. "Right, and the sheriff took over the shop. That was in sixty-six. But I had already cleared out and was bumming around Berlin, for in those days, according to the old custom, the fellow could arrest a defaulting debtor on the spot and jail him!"

"And it was just then that you came into the world, Oskar," said the mother.

"Yes, that was a terrible time," continued Eduard. "As big as the earth is, and as full of treasures, I myself didn't have a single red cent." Suddenly he laid his horny hand on his wife's arm. "And what harm did it do, after all, Mother? So we began again, on another street—with medical appliances and optical apparatus. I turned out that mist apparatus, as it was called, for showmen—you know, Oskar, those double projectors that make one picture disappear while another is appearing."

Oskar simply nodded. He had, after all, grown up in this world of light and optics.

"I tried everything in order to earn some money. Even the illuminated fountain in Kroll's establishment on the Königsplatz—I built that, Kroll's miraculous fountain, known all over the city. If there's even a spark of truth in what they say about heredity, you too will have ideas, all right."

Oskar Messter was hardly disturbed by the necessity of retrenching, of living modestly, in one room with a kitchen, behind the shop. The idea of improving his condition by increasing the sales of his appliances occupied his mind for only a few days; then it was pushed aside by his preference, inherited from his father, for seeking new things.

An optician named Busch, who sometimes stopped by in the evening and filled Messter's room with smoke from his mighty pipe, listened patiently to the impatience of his younger colleague. Now and then he yawned.

"Don't you ever get bored, Busch, always turning out the same things?"

Busch merely drew on his pipe.

"Don't you ever feel the desire to work out new ways of building new kinds of apparatus?" And, since Busch didn't answer, Messter went on: "Do you know what I dream about when I'm brooding away the days and nights here? I'd like to find something that would take me out of this mechanical execution of the same old routine jobs."

At that Busch took the pipe out of his mouth. "Everyone would like that! But to find it . . .?"

"One must simply keep one's eyes open."

But Messter had to wait a full year before something attracted his attention. Then, for the first time, he saw moving pictures, photographs, in a peep-show based on the principle of Anschütz's Rapid Viewer.

"Not bad!" he told himself. But, before he made up his mind to develop a similar apparatus, he must sternly suppress his urgent dreams and reflect, thoroughly, soberly, and realistically: How many times would the operation of such a device interest its owner before he became bored, put it to one side, and perhaps never used it again? He feared that it would have no great sale. And what about the possibility of developing it further? Messter saw none—and, what counted more, he felt none.

About that time Röntgen discovered the penetrating power of X-rays.

"Röntgen tubes! Look here, Busch, that's really something! Let's take that up!"

But Busch, as usual, was reserved.

"Just think how we could use that to increase the pulling

power of exhibitions at fairs! What an attraction it would be if the proprietor conjured up the shadow of his own skeleton on the screen or if he showed how much money everybody had in his pocket!"

Busch remained skeptical. "Do you really believe that people, for any length of time, would want to make their flesh creep with their own skeleton or their own death's-head?"

Messter reflected a while. "There's a rumor that even in medicine there may be some interest," he said, but he already sounded rather dejected.

Messter did begin production of what he called his Magic Boxes, which used X-rays, but the caution of the showmen, who thought the apparatus was too expensive, sobered him more than Busch's doubts. If he wanted to expand his business by means of novelties that really paid, he would have to seek further.

And he sought further, indefatigably! Until . . .

It was a beaming summer day, made to suit Berliners, who were seeking relaxation and hunting for merriment.

Even Messter was drawn outdoors. In front of Castan's Panopticon his interest was awakened by a group of people who were pressing forward toward a black box. It was only curiosity that led him to ask one of the group, "What is there to see?"

The stranger looked at him with unconcealed disdain. "You don't know Edison's Kinetoscope? You've never heard of it? Well, if you don't want to be an old fogy, just get in line. That's something you owe your education."

So Messter arrived at the massive box. He remained there for a long time. Again and again he ran through the scene in the American barbershop, the scene at the blacksmith's shop, and the scene in a saloon. He paid out many a twenty-pfennig piece.

In the evening a cheerful Messter returned to his home.

Even though he hadn't the faintest idea what was happening in the unwieldy box, he had the feeling that here was work for a skillful mechanic and for an excellent optician. But that was not all that made him cheerful. An indefinite feeling, a sixth sense, told him that the black monster had more than was apparent at first: the possibility of further development. These series of pictures not only presented the course of a short movement, as Anschütz's Rapid Viewer did, but showed fairly long scenes! And those could be entertaining—especially if one expanded them into little dramas.

But was that really possible? To judge of that, one must know the mechanism.

The next day he crept round the gigantic box at the Panopticon like a cat stalking a bird, but the box did not betray its secret. Messter had to go home, but he kept coming back, unwearied; Edison's Kinetoscope attracted him as a light attracts moths.

One day, at last, he was lucky. A man in a blue workman's blouse, whose sullen face betrayed his irritation, was just opening the box. Messter, overcome with curiosity, spied over his shoulders and saw that about sixty feet of film, pasted together into an endless band of pictures, ran over a complicated system of sprockets, or rollers, with little teeth, or spikes, at the ends. The teeth engaged holes punched regularly along the edges of the film. Messter, forgetting everything else, stuck his neck out still farther.

"Man, if I were you, I'd crawl right into the thing!" growled the repairman.

"Stuck again," answered Messter on the spur of the moment, as if this would excuse his curiosity.

"Again? The lousy box does nothing but stick!"

"Why?" asked Messter with the most innocent face.

"Why? Why?" The repairman unloaded all his wrath. "I'll tell you something, my dear sir: The whole trouble comes from the sharp teeth, which jab the celluloid instead of ducking into the holes. Anybody who knows his business ought to be able to see that! Besides"—the irritated man was no doubt glad to have someone to hear his complaints—"the material, the celluloid, is not strong enough. It can't stand the strain when the sprockets pull the strip along in jerks—forty times a second! Can you even imagine what that's like, young man?"

Messter strolled away—in an unusually exalted mood.

The exaggerated complaints of the man, his trouble with the sprockets, did not bother him. On the contrary, they showed him that here was a problem waiting for the ingenuity of a mechanic. What did bother him was the fact that only one person at a time could enjoy these pleasant little scenes. One must, if possible, have more spectators at a performance—perhaps even a full hall!

To find support for his idea, he called on his father. "The film transport must, of course, be improved," he said; "that is the first essential. Even after that is done, though, the cost of the individual performances is too high. The thing would pay if one could show the film to a large audience. The audience is there; the daily crowd in front of the Panopticon proves that."

The old mechanic looked over the steel frames of his glasses. "And how do you plan to do that?"

"By projecting the pictures on a wall—life size."

Eduard Messter shook his head. "That's quite a job!"

"But what a job! What an opportunity to develop the thing further!"

Oskar's eyes gleamed. No one could have understood that gleam better than Father Messter.

Messter holed up in his room and began calculating. At first he found that the illumination of each picture would have to take place within a ten-thousandth of a second. That seemed impossible to him, technically impossible. Hoping he had made a mistake, he did his figuring again; but even now the result he got seemed too short a time for adequate illumination of a picture. Too bad! The result involved him in a heroic mental struggle: however often and persistently he was tormented by the desire to find a way to project living photographs, he energetically suppressed it. He would have to abandon this new field of work.

Six months later Busch came to see him. Busch had been in Paris, and he told, between puffs on his pipe and as casually as he always did things, about the Lumière brothers, who had succeeded in projecting moving pictures on the wall.

Messter opened his mouth and forgot for a while to close it. He finally asked: "Is the short time allowed by the shutter enough, then, for a bright picture to be thrown on the wall?"

Busch, without even asking for a pencil, began to figure. "Let's assume that you have twenty-four pictures a second. The Lumière brothers are said to use fewer, but twenty-four is generally accepted as the normal number. Every picture would have, then, a twenty-fourth of a second. If we assume, further, that for half of that time the objective is covered by the shutter, to allow for the change of pictures, you will have about a fiftieth of a second for the illumination of each picture, and exactly the same time remains for the after-image, for the moment in which the spectators are really looking—without knowing it—at a dark blank wall."

"And I came out with thousandths of a second!" Messter frankly admitted.

"You certainly figured mighty badly there, my friend! Let's hope you do it only at the beginning and only with seconds! I really hope so. Idealists, in general, should be cautious with figures."

"Well, I've paid for my mistake: because of it I am too late with my glorious idea of projecting moving pictures." Immediately the dark cloud on his forehead disappeared. "But the apparatus for that must be built! Someone, after all, has to make the projectors!" After some reflection he added, "There's still that problem of the film transport, of the little spikes. How do the French take care of that?"

"Spikes? The Lumière brothers move the film along with a sort of claw . . . yes, I'd call it a claw."

Messter had a restless, almost sleepless night. The thought kept coming back to him that now it was really possible to exhibit living pictures to a hall full of people. His head burned, but cold sweat stood on his forehead. And the apparatus they used, what did it look like? That was the crucial question! Once, just once, he had to see that kind of apparatus—even if it were only for a second, only for a fiftieth of a second! And he must get hold of a piece of such a film! As poor in pocket as he was, as little time as he had left over from his work, as uncertain as the result might be, for this opportunity he would put everything else aside.

And then came that day in April 1896. One Rogulin, a Russian conjurer and showman, ordered from Messter, for his imposing amusement hall in Moscow, an X-ray apparatus with which to entertain his public in this most up-to-date way. Immediately following him—the two must have bumped into each other in front of the door—came that suspicious man who introduced himself as an impresario. He leaned secretively and fearfully over the counter and said right into Messter's ear: "I have heard that you are the most skillful optician for a long way round. And . . . and I am in great trouble."

He looked anxiously round to see if anybody was watching him. Then he took out from under his coat a condensing lens and laid it on the counter. "A repair job," he whispered. "It doesn't gather the light properly."

Messter looked doubtful. "I don't think I can do anything without the rest of the apparatus."

The stranger double-talked. "It's a tough situation! This lens belongs, you see, to a special apparatus, to an entirely new kind of apparatus for exhibiting . . . Look, it's not that

I don't trust you, you understand! The apparatus, developed by Robert Paul in London, is protected, anyway, by an English patent. Nevertheless, I have promised to guard its secret as the apple of my eye. Can you understand my exaggerated caution?"

"I can indeed; but then I can't help you."

"And we wanted to use the apparatus in the Winter Garden today!" He seemed to be inconsolable.

Messter merely shrugged regretfully.

Then the stranger had to give in.

An hour later Messter stood in front of the mysterious apparatus. What was it? He hardly trusted his eyes at first and pinched his ear to make sure that he was not dreaming. Then he gave a curious, thorough, and expert look at—a cinematographic projector. Two star-shaped wheels, to which seven radial slits gave the appearance of flowers, brought about the jerky forward movement of a film such as he had seen in Edison's Kinetoscope. Between them, and rotated by the crank, was a disk with two sturdy pegs, which turned the two stars with powerful shoves. Both stars were attached to a sprocket, which, as in Edison's apparatus, engaged the strip of film by means of two rows of little teeth, which fitted into the punched holes.

The exhibition in the Winter Garden was a complete failure. The impresario was not the only one who came out of it in a bad humor. There was, in fact, only one satisfied participant: Oskar Messter. The evening had brought him, besides his look into the projection apparatus, a piece of Kinetoscope film, which he had stipulated as the only compensation for his trouble—"as a souvenir," he said.

Messter ended this exciting and significant day with a decision that, though very simple, was to determine the rest of his life: what the Lumière brothers had accomplished in Paris, what Robert Paul had accomplished in London, that he, Oskar Messter, must accomplish in Berlin.

On the next day, in the room behind Messter's shop, a

projector began to grow—at a speed that revealed not only the skill but the frenzy of its creator. It was similar to the English model but surpassed it in performance. Nevertheless, in the new apparatus, too, the little teeth bit too sharply into the holes of the film. After the third trial Messter was convinced that this was the crucial problem. The change from picture to picture was too violent—too fast in the beginning and too fast at the end. In the camera that took the pictures the problem was not important, for a strip of film ran through the camera only once. But how could the film stand the strain if it was run through the projector again and again? No, this way of moving the film along would not do in a projector. The movement must be easier, softer. Then the perforation would not suffer, the film would not tear, the strip would not wobble so much, and the picture on the wall would not flicker so wretchedly.

Not much change was needed, apparently—only some little detail, perhaps only what would amount to a trick.

For cinematography, however, that trick was decisive.

Messter soon decided that one star-shaped wheel, with only five slits, was enough. Then the disk turned by the crank would need only one peg, but this peg must work wonderfully smoothly on the star-shaped wheel, so as to set it in motion slowly and softly.

Messter's task was to bring that about. He sat at his drawing board and designed, changed the radii and the angles, so that the circling peg should slide as smoothly as possible into each slit. He stood at his bench vise, sawed and filed, tested the result—and began all over again. The work cost him sweat and time—and all his savings.

His funds had reached a frighteningly low point when Rogulin, at the end of May, blustered into his shop. "Have you the apparatus, my dear Messter? . . . Wonderful!"

While Messter prepared the X-ray apparatus for delivery, the Russian told him, with highly colored enthusiasm, of the curiosity with which the people of Moscow were awaiting

the new Magic Box; but Messter, obsessed with the task that
had kept him awake for weeks, looked into the Russian's
sparkling eyes and asked: "What would you say offhand of
living photographs?"

The idea was a revolutionary novelty to Rogulin. Messter
told him about the exhibitions that were on view at several
places in Berlin, and the Russian, eager to see for himself,
spent the rest of the day going from show to show.

In the evening he turned up again at Messter's. He was
unreservedly enthusiastic. "My dear Messter, you have conquered my heart! Where can I get such apparatus?"

The mechanic, on the point of expressing his ignorance
with a shrug, suddenly comprehended this unique opportunity. His apparatus was not working to his own satisfaction, and his financial means were exhausted. If the Russian
bought his projector, he could begin again, avoiding all the
faults that bothered him.

He brought out his apparatus. "It may very well be the
only such apparatus available in Germany," he remarked
by the way.

Rogulin's enthusiasm was uncontrollable. He immediately
paid 1,900 marks for what was not only the first German
projector but the first really serviceable one.

The 1,900 marks worked miracles for Messter.

First he went to London to acquire new films for exhibition from Maguire & Baucus, English distributors of
Edison's films, which, until now, had been released only for
use with Edison's Kinetoscope. Having with some difficulty
acquired new films, Messter began to build his new projector
—with his own mechanism for intermittent movement, for
driving the film along in jerks. The wheel attached to the
sprocket that moved the film now had only four, instead of
five, radial slits. It reminded Messter so strongly of the cross
of the Knights of Malta that he always called it the Maltese
cross. Along the arcs between the slits, holding the Maltese
cross firmly in each of its fixed positions, rotated the circular

disk that was driven by the crank. At each whole turn the peg inserted in the disk slipped easily into a slit, pushed the Maltese cross, in a hundredth of a second, through a quarter turn, and then slipped quietly out of the slit as the disk, fitting closely into the next arc, held the Maltese cross firmly until the peg came round to the next slit for the next quarter turn of the cross. In order to begin and end the movement of the cross without a shock—and this was Messter's decisive idea— the peg, as it entered and left the slit, was moving along the lengthwise axis of the slit. Each quarter turn of the cross therefore began slowly and gently, gradually speeded up, gradually slowed down, and ended slowly and gently.

For this mechanism Messter received a patent. His Maltese cross, as it is still called, became the symbol of cinematography. (See the diagram on page 227.)

The invention of the Maltese cross—technically, without doubt, a decisive achievement—did not impress Messter himself especially. According to him, the idea had been lying there ready, and some day someone was bound to take it up. This someone happened to be named Oskar Messter. He was much more impressed by the fact that he had finally found the great new field of work of which he had long dreamed, and into that field he plunged with all the zeal of his enthusiastic heart. He built projectors and sold them rapidly—and not only in Germany. He used one of them to exhibit moving pictures himself in a hall on Unter den Linden. A competing exhibitor on the same street soon had to close down, despite his lower entrance fee, for his audience had become tired of constantly hearing the operator apologize because the film had torn or had been cut or had jumped out of its channel.

"You've done it, Messter," said Busch. "Your projector is first-class!"

It was characteristic of Messter that he was suddenly attacked, that very night, by anxiety—perhaps, indeed, as a result of Busch's praise. The anxiety was suddenly there, oppressive, frightening in the dark. Didn't his exhibitions depend on the willingness of the people in Paris and London to let him have films? And weren't all those unsuspecting people who had bought his projectors also dependent on a steady and sufficient supply of films? What if Paris and London decided some day to stop supplying the films? Who would then pay a single mark for a projector?

The anxiety grew and grew. It towered before Messter like an impregnable mountain and forced him to find a way round it. And he found a way—a way that only a man of action could have chosen: he would produce such films himself!

The requirements of such an enterprise immediately began to come to mind, one after another, like the links of a chain. Film production required the building of his own camera, required favorable conditions for taking pictures, required unexposed film (now called raw stock), required perforating machines that would work with great exactness, required the production of his own equipment for developing and fixing, of complicated machines for making prints from the negatives. Besides, the projector still needed improvement, especially in the film transport, and it needed accessory devices for rolling out and rewinding the film. He must also make appliances for cutting and pasting the film. And there was no reliable protection against fire! He had no experience with all these things, no models for them. The technically unexplored field seemed to Messter to extend to infinity, to have no boundaries—just as another such field seemed to Edison right after he invented the incandescent lamp. Before Messter lay not only a line of work but the task of a lifetime.

On the next day he took up that task—with a clear head, two strong hands, and an ardent spirit. Only one thing worried him: obtaining the raw stock. He could not himself produce that, too, besides all the other things! He applied, therefore, to the burgeoning German chemical industry, but without finding anything more substantial than good will.

He turned to the English representative of Kodak, telling him, with a certain pride, that he needed a large quantity of film. The representative answered by return mail: he was ready to make delivery, he said, but he politely called Messter's attention to Eastman's strict rule that he could deliver only for cash, and he figured the total cost of the order.

This letter gave Messter a shock. Even without looking at his account books he had no doubt that his financial reserves were exhausted. His experiments, and all the auxiliary equipment he had recently produced, had already used up more than his last cash. And, though someone might have been willing to lend money to Messter the mechanic, no one would lend to Messter the inventor, who seemed to have lost his bearings long before.

No, he simply could not meet King Kodak's conditions. And what did his realization of that mean? He forfeited all that he had created until then; his work, without Kodak's films, came to a stop, lost all value, was wasted—wasted time, wasted money—was nothing at all!

Days of torment followed in the now quiet workshop; the days crawled, the days were weary and burnt out.

And then, fortunately, Eastman, the all-powerful master of the Kodak film company, happened to visit Berlin. Messter saw his chance, and he did not let it pass. His energy and persistence carried him through, despite all the brusquely protective doorkeepers and coolly repulsing secretaries, to the master himself.

"You must grant me the credit, Mr. Eastman."

Eastman was all astonishment, mistrust, and reserve.

Messter's anxiety about his proud, far-reaching plans enhanced his eloquence miraculously. He spoke of his intentions and told how, without Eastman's help, they lost all their value. "And even if you have no sympathy for that, Mr. Eastman, you—you of all people—certainly must understand what it means to have to abandon one's life work." Messter felt, suddenly, that he could not move this stony fellow from Rochester. He calmed down; his voice sounded dull and resigned. "Excuse me! One becomes lost in one's own new world, sees only one's goal. Perhaps, after all, I aimed too high when, with the Maltese-cross drive, I took the first step into that new world."

The millionaire pricked up his ears. "We owe that drive to you?"

"Yes," answered Messter. "The patent is mine."

"Many people approach me, Mr. Messter, with all sorts of high-flying plans. They have taught me mistrust. But I have not lost my feeling for honest achievement, and you impress me. You have unlimited credit with me."

Messter was saved. The envious nudged one another with bitter smiles, and even his friends winked as they said, "So, Oskar's been lucky again." None of them, after all, had lived through the crisis with him.

Messter cranked out his first films—outdoors, of course, and that made difficulties. When he had finally got a scene all ready for the camera, the sun might disappear, perhaps not to reappear that day; or the light changed right in the middle of a scene. Or suddenly a wind came up. It seemed to rain only when he wanted to shoot a scene. In order to escape from these difficulties, he set up, on the fifth floor of his house, the first studio with artificial light—four arc lamps, each of which used up fifty amperes of current. The arc lamps were not an ideal solution of his problem, for the adjustment of the carbon rods was always breaking down, often during the most difficult scenes; but they were easier to control than the weather.

Here a great variety of films were produced, each about sixty feet long and running for about seventy-five seconds. Messter did everything himself: he wrote the script, directed the acting, supervised the camera work, developed, fixed, and cut the negatives, printed them, and projected the positives.

He now had to give his process a name. The Lumière

brothers had had the name Cinematograph registered as their
trademark, but Messter had plenty of names to choose from.
There were many more than a hundred names for the art
of making and projecting living pictures—a number that
was enough, by itself, to show how many people had been
trying at the same time to master the art. Messter chose the
name Kinetograph.

In October 1897 appeared his first catalogue, which listed
the films prepared for his Kinetograph. It began with enthusiasm: "Seldom, certainly, has any invention of recent
times been able to win the favor of the public so quickly and
to such a high degree as the Kinetograph, which makes real
events and actions visible; and seldom indeed has one touched
people's feelings so closely and held their interest so firmly!"
Then Messter numbered and listed his films.

No. 1 was described thus: "At the Brandenburg Gate in
Berlin: Animated street scene at noon on Unter den Linden
in Berlin; the columns of the Brandenburg Gate are visible in
the background."

Another: "Relaxation over Afternoon Coffee: The family
is sitting comfortably at the coffee table in the garden. The
youngest child is playing with a toy horse. Grandpa ties his
Great Dane to the table. The housewife pours coffee. Suddenly visitors appear. Grandpa stands up to greet them. The
Great Dane jumps after him and pulls over the coffee table
with all the dishes on it. (Humorous!)"

All his films showed much movement—or, more exactly,
showed joy that movement could be captured on the screen
at all.

Customers came to his hall on Unter den Linden and
snooped about with their partly inborn, partly new interest in
technical novelties. But they were content with having satisfied their curiosity. The expected crowds never came. Messter's daily intake at the hall, although he was showing films
from 10:00 A.M. to 11:00 P.M., varied between sixty and
seventy marks. Assuming that his Kinetograph was simply

not well enough known, he decided to advertise. He sent out cards bearing little transparencies: "Living photographs by means of the Messter Kinetograph, 21 Unter den Linden. Inventor and Manufacturer, Oskar Messter, 94-95 Friedrichstrasse, Berlin N.W., opposite the Central Hotel. Program for today: 1, Serpentine Dance; 2, Railways; 3, Street in Paris; 4, At the Seashore; 5, Troubled Sleep; 6, A Fast Painter."

The attendance did not improve.

Messter, with a shudder, remembered the days when, without any financial backing, he would have faced ruin if King Kodak had not happened to stop in Berlin. He mustn't get into that situation again. In 1900, with a heavy heart, he decided to separate his film operations from his optical shop, so that he would have at least a little something to fall back on.

He endeavored to find new ways of attracting the public. He enriched his exhibitions with phonographic recitations and performances of music. "Audible to all visitors along with the pictures" boasted his notices. He even hired a speaker to accompany the events flickering on the screen with the spriteliest possible, even witty, remarks.

The attendance fell off.

In 1903 his business reached such a low point that it seemed doubtful whether such an enterprise as the one on Unter den Linden could ever pay its way.

"You'd better close it down," advised the cautious Busch.

"But I need the hall—to demonstrate my apparatus if for nothing else."

"My wife says the poor attendance may be the fault of your repetition of comedy scenes. Show more timely, everyday things: fashion shows, races, life at court. That's the sort of thing people like to see."

Messter did show timely, everyday things. He exploited some of the astonishing possibilities of camera technique; he produced trick films. He could not win over the public.

In order to go on producing, he had to obtain funds. He

let a lawyer he knew take over a fifty-percent interest in his film business. "I will not leave in the lurch the man who invented the Maltese-cross drive, who created an essential element of our whole film industry," declared the lawyer patronizingly during the negotiations. He hoped, by the way, to make a considerable profit.

But the people who were expected to provide that profit failed to turn up. They didn't say why; they simply stayed away. They were, however, presented with an easily stated, easily understood reason for staying away when, at a charity bazaar in Paris, burning films, ignited by the explosion of an ether lamp, took the lives of seventy-three persons.

Messter's faith in cinematography was proof against all reproaches. "The casualties are to be deplored, of course," he said to the lawyer; "but in my eyes those people were the victims of a frivolous negligence that I have warned against from the beginning. Our technique provided adequate safety measures long ago. But who observes them?"

The lawyer made a face as if he had just bitten into a lemon. "Sometimes I regret that I put my good money into such a rotten business."

Messter brought his fist down on the table. "Sir, did anybody give up the idea of flying because Otto Lilienthal lost his life in one of his gliders?"

"You have an unusual way of consoling a person, Mr. Messter. I maintain, all the same, that the memory of the Paris fire will keep the public out of cinema theaters in the cities, no matter how well the safety precautions have been observed, and will ruin their prospects. The cinema is passing over to the sideshows, back to the annual fairs, where its predecessor, the magic lantern, dragged through its shabby career. And here we sit with towering debts. What have you to say to that?"

Messter didn't answer. He went home, closed the shutters of the shop, and locked the doors. He wanted to be alone, alone with his thoughts. Yes, of course, the lawyer was right. Films had become cheap trash for the fairs. Self-respecting people turned up their nose at the "flickers." Things had gone so far that one must apologize for still believing in cinematography.

And that was his life work?

The next day, early, he called on the lawyer. He was pale and worn from lack of sleep, but in his eyes was the glitter that his father had noticed and understood.

"I brooded a long time yesterday, very long. . . . Much has changed in the last few years. I used to be happy if the film rattled through the camera without complaining. The film was a strip of celluloid, and the whole thing was a technical miracle that people came in droves to wonder at. And we thought everything would stay that way. That was a mistake. I believe we must see things differently than we did in those days—ten years ago. People expect more. The 'Scenes from the Czar's Court,' the 'Nocturnal Hotel Scene,' the 'Kiss at the Masked Ball,' the constantly repeated pictures of people chasing people, all served up in five-minute portions—all that has left people disappointed. For them 'film' is no longer just that word they find in the English dictionary, no longer just the strip of celluloid that purrs off the reel; it is the symbol of the something new that they expected. So we must grip them where they want to be gripped—in their personal, human sympathies, not in their technical interests. We must make a film that doesn't depend on its novelty—already ten years old—that wins over its public, not by quack sideshow stunts or by the worn-out superlatives of circus posters, but by problems, scenes, and motives carved honestly and intelligently out of life itself. For something like that people will gladly give up two hours of their leisure. And I am going to make a film like that!"

"With what?" asked the lawyer. He played ostentatiously with a pile of unpaid bills.

"Even if I must scratch up the last penny myself, must beg for the last mark!"

A few days later, obsessed with his vocation and defying all obstacles, Messter began to shoot a film called *A Blind Girl's Success in Love*. The leading actress, named Henny Porten, was paid the star's fee of twenty marks.

The film went out to the exchanges, from them to the projectors in small theaters. It attracted attention, and many people called it a sensation. It was especially the distinguished acting of the attractive blonde in the leading role that excited the public. Many people wanted to know her name. One question kept pouring in: Wouldn't there soon be another film with that winning and fascinating actress? Yes, the public demanded such films!

Had Messter's convictions been justified?

For Oskar Messter the answer to this question no longer mattered. By that time he had already had to sell his share of his film business. The New Photographic Company—which, in the style that was soon to become common, called itself NPC—had bought him out.

Messter had withdrawn from a world that he himself had created.

Was his life's dream thereby dreamed out? Not if he still had the spirit of his father.

Eduard Messter was seventy years old when he ended a letter to his son with these words: "So bear the loss, and try, by new courage and iron energy, to win back what was lost. Think of the year 1866, when, by my blind confidence, I lost my steam-powered optical shop, and then, without a penny in my pocket, began again with your mother, through care and hunger, to establish a new life, and would not let myself be defeated by that fateful blow, and never rested until I had again accomplished something."

12.

THE PICTURES NEED SOUND

MIHÁLY followed the double line of blooming chestnut trees along the broad avenue. He felt peculiarly refreshed. The Prater, with its tender, slightly melancholy mood, had thoroughly deadened his painful longing for his Hungarian homeland.

And now? What to do?

Most of his high-spirited countrymen would not have found it hard, here in Vienna in 1913, to put together a program of evening pleasures that would be worthy even of Dénes von Mihály. But he had other interests, and that was why he had taken, on a side street, seclusive lodgings that certain people could not stick their noses into—people who only made jokes about things they didn't understand. And so that he could, if necessary, communicate quickly with his superiors, he had, mounted on the wall, one of those monstrous wooden boxes for telephoning.

Before he considered any plans for the evening, he had really made up his mind to visit Father Krause's again. That was the place—if he didn't happen, at the time, to prefer rummaging among second-hand books—where he had always found the best relaxation. He looked down with amusement at his civilian clothes. Wasn't that why he had changed from his uniform? Father Krause would certainly faint if a uniformed lieutenant of hussars entered his Cinema.

Without hesitation Mihály turned to the right, entered the amusement park, and sauntered through it, stopping now and then at an entertainment booth, until he reached his goal. The barker, Krause's son August, was doing his pitch in front of a gigantic placard on which the artist had squandered much imagination and even more garish color: a cowboy, wearing a slouch hat, was running amuck and had just shot the man standing near him. Against this background Mrs. Krause's tired old woman's face, under her unkempt gray hair, seemed especially colorless. She had charge of the ticket booth. Over all soared a bold arch made out of shipping-case covers, on which were fixed heavy black letters: KRAUSE CINEMA.

"Just come closer, ladies and gentlemen," roared August, whose voice was raw and hoarse, "and step right in. Continuous performance! You will see here what you have never yet seen: living pictures. The Cinema! You will see here the most amazing and most amusing thing the world has ever seen: a genuine American film from the Wild West. You will be gripped and touched, you will laugh and cry. Children and the military pay half price. And then there is the rest of this rich program: a fashion show in Paris, the London Peace Conference reopened. And finally the most delightful of these delights: "Philip in a Tight Spot." You will laugh till you cry. One sensation follows another. Step in!"

He nodded familiarly as Mihály went past him to the ticket booth.

"Satisfied, Mother Krause?" asked Mihály.

"Business could be better, Lieutenant," complained the old woman. "There's too much propaganda against us; you would think we were running the most disreputable place in the city. I think the theaters are to blame, and the tavern-keepers: they're afraid of losing their customers. Many people come here only after dark, hoping they won't be recognized. And the expenses—only the expenses—keep going up. And now, as you know, we have to pay a pianist. It was cheaper, more sensible, when my husband simply explained the different scenes; everything went well then. But today we have to have music, Lieutenant. The people demand it."

Mihály laid two twenty-heller pieces in the glass saucer. "Hearing it through the wall this way, I don't think it sounds like Horak."

"No, a substitute is playing today. Mr. Horak's wife has just had another child—a boy. He's to be named Peter, and the baptism is today."

The substitute at the piano threatened to shiver the plank walls, now with Fučik's "Entrance of the Gladiators," now with the overture to Herold's *Zampa*. The lusty fellow regarded these two pieces as the best background music for films; they were, besides, his whole repertory.

"He plays a little loud, don't you think so, Lieutenant? And we haven't yet paid for the piano."

The officer grimaced with pain. "And on top of all that he doesn't seem to be used to playing in the dark. He often hits the wrong keys."

Mrs. Krause shrugged. "How can you get a good pianist today? All the movie houses swallow them up."

Mihály sat down in one of a row of wobbly seats that were held together by a strip of wood running along the backs. Behind him a deep voice was murmuring to a girl, in front of him a woman was crackling a stiff paper bag, and on the screen was "Philip in a Tight Spot." It was the usual film of pursuit. Philip, this time a young chimneysweep, had, for a change, pilfered an apple. But the cause of what followed really made no difference; all that counted was how much damage the fleeing Philip and the pursuing market woman could cause before the wild chase ended in a confused tangle and one could no longer make out who was beating whom.

After the Paris fashion show the drama from the Wild West flickered over the screen. The film, which was wretchedly worn, tore three times and made the substitute pianist lose all self-control. When, true to the garish placard outside, the hero went to work exterminating all around him, the bass voice behind Mihály roared pitilessly: "Don't forget that piano-player; he deserves it most of all."

Father Krause turned on the lights and announced that police regulations required that the place be ventilated. Perhaps he would not have observed the regulation so conscientiously if he had not been hankering after his pipe. Mrs. Krause wound the films back while he took her place in the ticket booth. He turned to Mihály.

"If everything goes well, Lieutenant, this wooden shack will soon disappear. And Father Krause too. The gentleman who has been after me for a long time—a fine gentleman, by the way—bought the place from me this morning, just as it is." He patted his breast pocket with satisfaction. "In there is the certified check. And I didn't let it go cheap." After a pull on his pipe he added: "There are always suckers."

"What makes you think this man is one?"

"The fool is sure that he will soon make so much profit on the long films now being made in Denmark and Italy that he'll be able to tear down this shack and put up a brick building that will satisfy even the latest police regulations. He imagines that the future belongs to films." He drew thoughtfully on his pipe. "I ask you, Lieutenant, to whom and to what hasn't the future belonged? I have a different idea of the future. There's too much talk of war for me—much too much! Since we occupied Bosnia in 1908, the Balkans have always been in turmoil. The situation gets worse all the time. And if things really break loose, there's the end—for the Krause Cinema too, whether it's wood or brick."

"But you know yourself, Father Krause, how much rumor and journalistic gossip there is in all that talk of war. And I don't share your skepticism about the future of the cinema."

"Ten years ago, Lieutenant, when curiosity was drawing people here in swarms, you might have convinced me. Even five years ago! But today? You see yourself how the attendance is slackening off. All right, we simply have different views about that. Only don't express your view too openly before my wife; she has always imagined that we'd be giving up God knows what if we sold this shack."

"Well, what does she say now that you have sold it?"

Krause became strictly confidential. "She doesn't suspect it yet. I'm waiting for a while—for the right moment. Right now I haven't got the courage to tell her."

"Oh, dear!" Mihály scratched behind his ear. "That looks like an unpleasant discussion ahead of you. Well, I'll be interested in hearing how it comes out."

"I'll tell you about it, Lieutenant; you can depend on it. Oh, yes, there's another thing: I got a job for August out of the bargaining. He'll no longer stand at the door roaring like a wild bull. He'll sit comfortably in the projection booth, beside the apparatus—as operator."

"Just a moment!" Mihály cut him short as he pointed toward the more pompous film theater that stood nearer the great circular plaza. "Do you see the man who is slinking out of the cinema there?"

Krause leaned far forward, but he shook his head.

"Never mind, Father Krause; you wouldn't see anything of him even if the wall were not in your way. The coward has turned his coat collar up so high that even the end of his nose hardly sticks out. But I'll bet you anything you want that it's my neighbor. He's one of those who turn up their noses at films—in the daytime, and in respectable company. But I'll catch the rogue!" Waving good-night to Krause, he hurried toward the plaza.

The two men had reached the center of the plaza when Mihály tapped the rogue on the shoulder. The muffled-up man turned round with a start, then said: "Oh, it's you, Lieutenant!"

"I merely wanted to take the liberty of asking, Doctor, whether you liked the living photographs."

What could be seen of Dr. Kettel's face resembled that of a schoolboy who has been caught stealing apples. "You certainly don't suppose that I . . ."

"Now, now," said the officer reassuringly; "you don't need to feel embarrassed before me, Doctor. I am no better than you."

The face of Dr. Kettel, government official, relaxed and then assumed a plump, somewhat embarrassed smirk. "I happened to have two hours . . . between other things . . . free time! . . . What can one do with two hours? . . . I thought . . . just for relaxation, for distraction . . . For that purpose, after all, these proscribed cinematographs are good, are well suited . . ."

"Yes, yes, but what I don't understand is how people can praise something as an unprecedented advance in technology and then restrict it to sideshows and refuse to accept it in good society."

"That's exactly my opinion, Lieutenant!" A wave of harmony carried them across the plaza. "But I believe, I really believe, there may be a change. It's true, it's taking people an amazingly long time to create out of this gift of technology an instrument that will be useful to all, entertaining to all. But the outlines of the future development can already be seen. The inventors are already receding into the background, and the producers of films are pushing themselves into the foreground."

They strolled along the street on which they lived, occasionally standing still and forming an obstacle to the spring-happy bustle on the sidewalk. "The French," continued the Doctor, "especially Pathé and Gaumont, rule the world market with their films, in which they exploit not only world literature but Max Linder's unsurpassable humor. The Italians, on the other hand, bid for attention with their spectacular films, with fascinating mass scenes. *Quo Vadis*, which you have surely seen, is said to have cost only 50,000 lire but to have earned its producers many millions from Germany and England, France and America. What a success! What an incentive! What a temptation, Lieutenant!"

Mihály merely nodded.

"Even Messter was able to save himself. And why? Because he found the bridge leading from inventor to producer. A symbol of his time! Yes, he too learned that everything depends on what one offers people and how one offers it, that the content of the film is what counts—and the direction. Within a year he was able to buy back all his shares, and today the Messter Film Company, Inc., is right on top. His films starring Henny Porten have been an unbroken series of successes: *The Children's Doctor, The Maid, Two Women, Imprisoned Souls, Claudie of the Geiserhof, Fairy Hands, Countess Kitchen-fairy* . . ."

Mihály laid his hand soothingly on the other's arm. "That's enough. I see that you are very well informed."

"And do you know what's especially remarkable about his rise? That he owes his beginning to the modest little sum of 1,900 marks, which some Russian or other once paid him for a projector! It's amazing when one reminds oneself what one can do with 1,900 marks! Isn't that so?"

"Truly amazing." Mihály remained standing expectantly under an arc lamp. "And so . . .?"

"Yes, more and more people keep coming to the cinema. And there will be still more and more! Workingmen are fighting for an eight-hour day and Sundays off. And they will get both, for some day it will become clear that the advance of mechanization, the constantly growing use of machines, will finally relieve mankind of its burdens. This development will bring more leisure to millions—and more interest in the cinema. More interest means greater attendance, increased earnings, for—for the mass entertainment of the future. Come, don't you think so?"

"More or less. At the moment, however, I am simply astonished to find a government official venturing on such trains of thought."

Dr. Kettel ignored the mockery. He even slipped his arm under Mihály's elbow with a familiarity that the officer found excessive. "I shall trust you, Mihály, with a secret that explains a good deal. I have inherited a little money—nothing big, but still . . . something. Naturally one wants to put one's money into what will bring one the greatest profit. And so, I reflected, how would it be to invest my capital in a cinema theater?"

The lieutenant of hussars whistled sharply. He began to understand. "So that's why you have been so absorbed in this whole problem, from the director to his audience of working-men—whose leisure you have even included in your calculations!"

"Exactly! And I've gone even further: I've considered what the profit must be if one produces such a film oneself."

Mihály—he had suddenly had enough of the rogue—plucked at the turned-up coat collar. "And would that activity be suitable to one of your rank, Doctor?"

"Really, Mihály"—Dr. Kettel laughed so heartily that passersby turned and looked after him—"when even Count Sascha Kolowrat condescends to found his own film company! He has his own studio on Biber Street. Recently, moreover, I have heard that his company is even planning to build in Sievering. What do you say to that?"

"I am glad to hear that you have such reassuring information. But one question occurs to me: What special knowledge do you have for such an undertaking?"

"Must one really understand something about the business, Lieutenant? In America a half-dozen men are supposed to have gone directly from the clothing industry—and ready-made clothes at that!—into the film industry—because they figured that entertainment would yield higher profits than clothing."

"Right! And I have also heard that in those circles it's not considered a disgrace if such an expert orders ten pounds of perforation."

Dr. Kettel gave an ear-shattering laugh. "So you see! And you demand miracles of me? You'd better follow my example: if you can spare a few pennies, stick them into films!"

Mihály rocked his head reflectively. "Let me look over the situation first. Film! Film! Human beings, wrapped in the magic darkness of the theater, succumb to the double fascination of the screen: light and movement. Either by itself would be enough to captivate people. Think of all the spectators who have been gripped by religious rituals in caves, temples, and churches, by colorful performances in theaters, by bloody hunts in the arena." He let the Doctor step first through the house door. "And yet how tame were all those spectacles compared with the urgency of the flickering screen! How powerful are the means with which the cinema works! Just think of the close-ups! Do you believe that the Romans saw the dying of gladiators as vividly as spectators at the cinema do through the close-up?"

Kettel wanted to stop and ask a question, but Mihály did not give him a chance. "And this effect—we mustn't forget, Doctor—is achieved in the strangest way. By means of a few grams of silver artfully embedded in gelatin, men are so shaken or so moved to laughter that they never notice that for half of the time they are staring at a dark, blank wall. Grotesque, isn't it? Have you ever stopped to think, by the way, that only a few of these silver atoms wander—or, more exactly, change their positions almost unnoticeably from one frame to the next—when joy is transformed into sorrow, love into hate, good will into envy? Isn't it frightening to realize with what cheap means the thinking and feeling of human beings can be permanently influenced today?" They were standing before the door to Mihály's apartment when the officer pointed his index finger at Kettel's chest like a revolver. "And that influence is exercised by men who, in your opinion, Doctor, need show no qualifications but an intractable inclination to make money."

"That's an ususual way of looking at things."

"I am, first of all, a technician."

Dr. Kettel seemed to be struck by lightning. "Technician? You, an officer?"

Mihály opened the door and with a gracious gesture invited his neighbor to enter. "If you want to be convinced of that by a look into my world, please come in!"

Kettel could not have said which surprised him more at that moment, Mihály's startling avowal of technical knowledge or his unexpected invitation. Taken completely by surprise, he entered, and he immediately missed, in the small room, the well-known military orderliness. Piles of books lay here and there, thick rollers, narrow strips of film. Eder's *Yearbook of Photography* lay open as if it had claimed the officer's most recent attention. On two small tables were crowded bits of apparatus that meant nothing at all to Kettel, and chemicals at which he sniffed mistrustfully.

"You see that I *have* stuck a few pennies into the cinema," said Mihály, offering his guest a comfortable armchair. "But let us forget these puzzling things, about which you don't want to know anything anyway."

"You are unfair," said Kettel defensively. "It's just that I was convinced that technology had already contributed its share to the cinema."

"Your judgment is flattering, and laymen fall easily into such heresies. May I call your attention to a few deficiencies of cinematography?" Mihály adopted a fatherly air. "Just one example: Haven't you ever missed color in the cinema, Doctor?"

"Color?"

"Our world is, after all, gay and many-colored! Has your

assiduous attendance at the cinema so dulled your senses that for you the sky is really gray, and a smiling mouth really black? Or do you now enter film theaters only in order to increase the attendance?"

Kettel fidgeted uncomfortably in his chair. "Is it possible, then, that . . .?"

"Yes, indeed! The first producers of films, such as Pathé and Gaumont, whose senses were not yet so dulled as ours, even tried to get round the deficiency. They dyed whole reels of film. The technique of the time did not allow them to do any more. The color followed the mood of the scene: blue for gruesome nocturnal scenes, yellow for cozy tea parties. When people got tired of such trash, the producers tried a more refined method: a battalion of young girls ruined their eyes coloring the tiny figures in those little pictures, each as big as a postage stamp. Today we hope to find another way. Chemistry, that new magic, shall help us. A so-called accident—really an unusual power of observation—showed the way to a German professor of chemistry some forty years ago. He was named Vogel, by the way." The Lieutenant was silent a moment. "But perhaps—with your peculiar point of view—you are bored by what I am telling you."

"You will probably smile, but I should be very much interested if"—Kettel suddenly hissed like an irritated tiger—"if you could manage to leave off your sarcasms."

"Let's come to an agreement, Doctor: as long as you try to take cinematography seriously, I shall be glad to take you seriously."

The hussar poured two glasses of wine—as if he felt obliged to make a conciliatory gesture. One he shoved across the table. Then he leaned back comfortably in his armchair, like one who is thinking of indulging in pleasant memories. "I suppose you know that the original photographic emulsions were not equally sensitive to all colors of the spectrum. Blue and violet had more effect than other colors. Red, on the other hand, had no effect at all; it showed in photographs only as black spots. That was the time when ladies were careful not to appear before a camera in red dresses; and it was at that time that Professor Vogel, with admirable acuteness, realized that the emulsion becomes especially sensitive to certain colors if certain dyes are added to it. I shall explain to you what happens by a specific example. An emulsion dyed blue appears blue to us because it absorbs yellow, its complementary color, to a greater degree than other colors. That means, however, that such an emulsion, which absorbs especially yellow, must be especially sensitive to yellow. As the specialist says, it has been sensitized to yellow. Or—another way of saying the same thing—a plate dyed blue will record, in a landscape, only what is yellow."

He filled the glasses again, thinking it necessary to grant Kettel a short pause for reflection.

"Following this basic idea, one added to the emulsion, in definite relative amounts, sensitizers that enabled it to respond to the different colors in proportion to their degrees of brightness. Thus we got the so-called color-true plates, which are known in the trade as orthochromatic plates."

Mihály, lost in his thoughts, leafed through Eder's *Yearbook of Photography*. "And then came Frederick E. Ives, an American, living in Philadelphia. Twenty years after Vogel's revolutionary discovery he tried to use it to produce color photographs. He began with the fact, long known, that you can mix any color you want with the three primary colors, red, green, and blue. Ives argued as follows: If I take a picture of a landscape three times, one right after another, with three plates, each of which has been sensitized to one of the three primary colors and correspondingly dyed, I shall get three pictures, a red one, a green one, and a blue one, each of which, of course, will reproduce only certain parts of the landscape. If I then combine the three plates, I shall have a picture with all the colors of the landscape. This is true, you must remember, only if I look at the picture by light

that passes through the plates; that is, it is true for transparencies. But that's what film pictures are. All this is, of
course, easier said than done. The trouble begins with the
sensitizers and doesn't end with them. For the problem immediately becomes much more difficult when you try—and
it's obviously the next thing to do—to get all three emulsions
on one carrier. Can you imagine how vaporishly thin the
emulsions must be for this purpose? And they must not, remember, flow into one another. A single person can hardly
master such problems." His right hand seemed to wipe out the
past. "It cost me much money, still more time, and many
sleepless nights before I came to that realization."

Kettel's hawk-like face pushed forward. "What, you
worked at the problem yourself?"

"Didn't the disorder surrounding you tell you that?"

"But—well, after all, you are an officer!"

The lieutenant of hussars shrugged. "Don't be upset; there
are even supposed to be men who can knit. Anyway, you
will now understand that my point of view on the cinema
is different from yours. Perhaps it would be advisable for you
to strengthen yourself with a swallow of wine for what is to
come. I gave color photography up, you see, when I realized,
in an access of exemplary self-knowledge, that neither my
chemical experience nor my limited opportunities were what
the problem required. My next ambition was to give the
cinematic image a plastic—you might say a three-dimensional
—form."

Kettel accompanied his dumbfounded look with inarticu-
late gurgling.

"Yes, there is such a thing. Many people consider the
lack of spatial depth a special defect of the cinema. For
ordinary photography the problem was solved long ago by
stereoscopic exposures made with two adjacent objectives.
This double picture, consisting of two pictures that are a
little different from each other, are viewed in a special frame,
in which they look three-dimensional. The method is very

suitable to our sense of space but cannot, unfortunately, be easily extended to every spectator in a cinema theater."

"And you?"

"I really came upon this problem through color photography. One can, you see, achieve the plastic effect with two pictures of different colors. It is customary to make one red and the other green. The two pictures are slightly displaced in relation to each other, are printed one over the other, and are viewed through red-green glasses, so that each eye—as with the stereoscope—sees only one picture. You can get such pictures in two colors, with the necessary glasses, in any stationery store. This technique can actually be used in the cinema, but holding or wearing the two-colored glasses would upset the contemplative calm of our indolent spectators. I don't think it's the final solution. I believe, rather, that a great many more people will break their teeth on this problem. Yes, I feel sure that the three-dimensional cinema will need quite different and much more expensive apparatus."

"And the present investments will become worthless? Frightful!" Unconcealed anxiety appeared on Kettel's face.

"On that point I can reassure you. Your anxiety is exaggerated. The plastic cinema will not be here for some time yet. Before that we'll give the film sound."

"Mihály, I don't know whether you are serious or are pulling my leg!"

"With that idea, too," the Lieutenant continued, "I am not original. Edison, indeed, really began work on sound film before true cinematography existed. His attempts failed because he didn't succeed in synchronizing picture and talking machine perfectly. But there was still a demand for sound—if only in order to drown out the racket made by the projector. For the present a strong pianist who hammers away relentlessly is the best solution. I have nothing against pianists, you understand; I simply think that the events on the screen should have a better background. I have my own plan, which is not original, to be sure, though it does depart from

Edison's way. I am following in the footsteps of Ernst Ruhmer, who wanted to photograph sounds."

"Photograph sounds!"

"My instinct tells me that this technique would be the most suitable for photographed scenes. I'm thinking of a sort of 'projectophone,' of projected sound."

"Now you are straining my powers of imagination."

"You don't need your imagination, for I can show you something of the process." He walked over to the table beside the telephone and shoved a few pieces of apparatus to one side. In the open space he set up a tripod, from which a small circular mirror hung by a silk thread. Attached to the bottom of the mirror was a coil of wire. "I borrowed this set-up from Arthur Korn, the master of phototelegraphy. It's a fact that we inventors live by the new things we take from one another! Korn has the coil oscillate in a strong magnetic field." He rolled a powerful ring-shaped magnet forward. "According to the size and rhythm of the current flowing through it, the coil is turned through the magnetic field. It carries the mirror with it. A beam of light falling on the mirror is made to dance—just as it is by boys who use a mirror to annoy their elders. I can photograph the oscillating beam of light at the wall there—on a moving strip of film." He pointed past the telephone to a black box. "The vocal impulses that I produce with this microphone"—his sinewy hands reached quickly over the table—"must in this way produce a complex zigzag line—much like those you have no doubt seen in the automatic recording apparatus of a weather station. But here begin the great difficulties. The variations in the current are too slight to give the needed impulse to the coil and the mirror. The current will have to be strengthened."

Absorbed in his subject, he had not noticed until now that Kettel was staring fixedly through the window. "Perhaps it is already too late to arouse in you the right sort of interest in the cinema," growled Mihály bitingly.

"Excuse me, but I was bothered by that glow above the Prater. It looks as if there might be a fire there."

Mihály didn't even bother to look. "Probably a sideshow proprietor is promoting his new attraction by an especially extravagant use of light. Electricity leads one into that temptation. And I feel the lack of generated current here," he complained with a comical pretense of helplessness. Although Dr. Kettel could not forgo staring through the window, he smiled at the inventor's unconcealed obsession.

At that moment the telephone rang. Dénes von Mihály, almost solemnly, lifted the heavy receiver from the long brass hook. "Oh, it's you, Father Krause! What's that you say? . . . Really? . . . Completely? . . . Well, that was certainly a unique opportunity to tell your wife that you had sold it. Yes, I agree with you there. . . . No, you didn't disturb me. I am glad that you kept your promise. . . . I'll run into you again soon. . . ." He put the receiver back on its hook, turned the magneto crank, and returned to his apparatus.

"The glow that you noticed earlier, Dr. Kettel, does really come from a fire. Krause's Cinema is in flames."

"What's that you say? Oh, what a calamity!"

"Krause doesn't feel that way about it. He had sold the place, you see. The buyer—the fool, as Krause calls him—practically forced the money on him this morning. That's fate!" Hearing no answer, he looked at his guest. Kettel had collapsed, a mass of misery, in Mihály's armchair.

"Don't you feel well, Doctor?"

"Not well! That's putting it mildly! I was that fool."

The officer rubbed his nose. "Well, if you should need a swallow, to fortify yourself, the bottle is within your reach."

Three years later—in 1916, while World War I was ravaging Europe—Dénes von Mihály, captain of hussars, registered a Hungarian patent on a "writing mirror" with which he inscribed sound vibrations on a strip of photographic film.

13.

THE SOUND TRACK

IN THE late autumn of 1918, when World War I had come to an end, many men were compelled to make a new place for themselves in a peaceful Germany. Joseph Massolle and Hans Vogt, mechanics and good technicians, and Dr. Josef Engl, a physicist, were among them. It seemed obvious at first that they should look for suitable positions in some industrial plant. But the army of disarmed, returning soldiers was huge—too big for industries that first had to reorganize for new fields of work.

The three ambitious men then decided to pool their resources and talents. Even though they had little in worldly goods, their savings would help them through the beginning. They were, moreover, used to going hungry. Most of those around them were going hungry. Since the postwar turmoil encouraged speculation, they would certainly find a backer if they were successful, and they believed in their eventual success.

One question was still not settled: In what field should they work?

After full consideration they decided to add sound to the

motion picture. They knew very well that their idea was not original. Rumors of it had been flying about for decades. And, if one admitted the truth, the sound film had really existed a long time before the silent film had conquered the world. Edison had created it even before the cinematographic apparatus had developed into its final form. After him Messter in Germany, Pathé and Gaumont in Paris, and many others, too, had taken up the problem. All of them, following Edison's example, tried to unite the phonograph and the projector; and all of them struggled with the same difficulty: synchronizing the phonographic sound with the picture on the screen. And all—so far—had failed. The movie producers drew their conclusions: they entrusted all explanation of the story shown on the screen to the subtitles—short lines of explanation or dialogue, which interrupted the action; and each theater had to provide the necessary accompaniment of sound according to its means—perhaps with an orchestra, at least with a pianist.

The silent film had won.

It would have been ridiculous, however, to believe that people had finally abandoned their desire for a natural completion of the picture by means of sound. Weren't there other, more promising possibilities than phonographic sound?

Engl, Vogt, and Massolle reasoned that, if they wanted to unite picture and sound intimately, they could do so only on the strip of film. If they wanted to impress the sound on the light-sensitive emulsion of the film, they could do so only with light; they must produce photographic sound.

They threw themselves into that task with all their energy.

While Vogt and Massolle began to assemble the necessary tools and equipment for the laboratory they rented in Berlin-Wilmersdorf, Engl brought his scientific knowledge up to date by studying all the recently published reports that had any bearing on their plans.

Ernst Ruhmer, a German physicist, was undoubtedly the

first who had tried to photograph sound on film. That was near the beginning of the century, and he had pursued a train of thought that apparently went back to Alexander Graham Bell: he transformed the sound waves of the voice, by means of a microphone, into a varying electric current; used that current to vary the light of an electric arc; and photographed the varying light on a strip of moving film. Since his film moved much faster than motion-picture film, he was probably not thinking of combining his recorded sound with motion pictures. The principle was clear, and thereafter the purpose of research was to find the best ways of doing three things: (1) transforming the microphone's variations of current into variations of light; (2) recording the variations of light on a moving strip of film; (3) transforming those variations of light back into variations of current that would drive a loudspeaker.

Most investigators hoped to satisfy the first two requirements by a system based on a coil attached to a mirror and rotating in a strong magnetic field.

Engl kept on searching. He came upon the work of S. A. Berglund, a Swede; of E. A. Lauste, a Frenchman, who, after working some years for Edison, had actually made a crude sound-on-film motion picture but had not been able to carry his work further; of Arthur Korn, who had found a way to send photographs by telegraph wire and was seeking a way to send them by wireless telegraphy; and upon the Hungarian patent issued to Dénes von Mihály, who had made a beam of light reflected from the mirror attached to a turning coil oscillate with the rhythm of his voice. And this dancing beam of light, exposing a passing strip of film, was supposed to produce the same sort of zigzag line as the pen of a recording thermometer—a sort of fever curve of human speech!

Engl was eager to begin his own experiments, but he had to wait until the necessary equipment had been scraped together. And then, when the laboratory was finally ready, the three inventors were not satisfied with the mirror's zigzag writing. How were they to reproduce the original sounds from that?

Engl went on seeking. He began to have more confidence in those who photographed, not the dancing beam of light, but the quantity of light passing through a narrow slit, which varied as the mirror turned and thus produced on the passing film a continuous streak, now mostly light, now mostly dark, according to the delicate sound vibrations.

The three men were not spared the hours of doubt that afflict every researcher. Why was it that most of the clever men who had engaged in this work before them had not tried to apply the photographed sounds to the cinema? Were they themselves running into a blind alley? Or was this a repetition of that grotesque situation of a hundred years before when many were studying the sensitivity to light of various materials, especially of the silver salts, without turning them to photographic use?

They put their heads together over these problems for hours at a time, for whole nights at a time.

At last they imagined that they understood what the main problem was: the streak on the film, with its wavering line between light and dark parts, must be turned back into sound loud enough to fill a large, even a very large, hall. For that purpose only the photoconductive cell was generally known and readily available. Certain substances—selenium, for example—have the peculiar property of changing their electrical resistance when the intensity of the light falling on them changes. The next thing to do, obviously, was to illuminate such a photoconductive cell with a strong light passing first through a slit and then through the black-and-white sound track.

If they wanted to put the sound track on the normal strip of film, they would have to narrow the image size established by Edison. They decided that a band about two millimeters wide was the most that they could chisel off the width of the picture. One dimension of the rectangular slit, its length, was thereby determined. What about the other? All three men were convinced that a true reproduction of sound required as narrow a slit as possible, so that the high tones, with their many thousands of vibrations per second, should not be suppressed. If they made the slit only one millimeter wide, however, they would have only a tiny window, one by two millimeters. They wondered whether the small quantity of light passing through such a tiny slit would change the resistance of the photoconductive cell sufficiently to produce variations of current great enough to drive a loudspeaker.

Perhaps that was the hurdle that the others had not been able to jump.

They began their experiments. They acquired a photoconductive cell that was supposed to be, in its light-sensitive layer, the latest achievement of technology, and they illuminated it with a strong lamp through the sound track that ran beside the pictures of a strip of film. They connected the cell and one of the usual loudspeakers of the time—a greatly enlarged telephone receiver—to a source of current. As the wavering light varied the resistance of the cell, variations of current must vibrate the diaphragm of the speaker, and these vibrations must be audible—at least as a crackling.

But the loudspeaker did not utter a sound.

Not even an especially sensitive telephone receiver revealed the slightest vibration.

"Just about what we expected," growled Massolle.

They sat, heavily disappointed, among their artfully arranged instruments.

"But the variations of current must be there!" Engl insisted.

"They are probably too small for us to detect."

"Then we must amplify them."

Amplify them? Neither Edison nor Messter had been able to do that. Since the perfection of the electron tube, however, which had been greatly developed and improved by its use in wireless telegraphy and especially by the demands made on it during the recent war, there had been a way to amplify electric currents a thousand times, even a million times. The principle was simple—once it had been discovered. The ends of two wires, the cathode and the anode, were fused into an almost completely evacuated glass bulb, the so-called tube. If an electric potential was set up between them, electrons, the smallest units of electricity, passed at terrific speed from the cathode to the anode; that is, an electric current flowed through the tube (Fleming's diode). If a fine wire mesh, called the grid, was put between the cathode and the anode (as in De Forest's triode, which he named the Audion), the stream of electrons passing from cathode to anode could be controlled by an electric potential applied to the grid, much as the passage of light through a window is controlled by a venetian blind. The important point was that the control could be exerted even by very slight changes of the grid potential: the slightest variations controlled great streams of electrons between cathode and anode; that is, the tube could greatly amplify the electric impulses directed to the grid.

Wireless telegraphy had been using such amplifying tubes for some time. If they were to be used for sound films, a suitable circuit would first have to be designed.

The three inventors tried different circuits: they varied the resistance, changed the grid potential, soldered wires with the greatest care and the next day connected them differently. And now and then, holding their breath, they listened at the telephone receiver. No mother could have awaited more eagerly the first babbling of her child. And success came at last.

For their new resistance circuit the three men received, on April 17, 1919, their first patent, No. 350,999.

But they were not satisfied. Speech was not reproduced clearly enough to suit them.

Engl thought the slit used in the exposure of the film was too wide. Vogt thought the variations in the light passing through the film to the photoconductive cell were too slight because the variations in the sound track of the exposed and developed film were too slight. Massolle thought the loud-speaker was too sluggish.

They had years of work ahead of them, and they looked fearfully at their dwindling savings. Oh, well, once they were successful . . . They agreed to try first to improve the production of the sound track.

Engl took up Arthur Korn's idea of using the glow lamp, which, though rather highly evacuated, had not such a high vacuum as the electron tube. Even a weak current covered the cathode with what looked like a furry skin of light, and this light had an extraordinarily strong effect on the light-sensitive emulsion of films. And the skin of light itself was remarkably responsive to variations in the current: if the current decreased a little, the skin of light shrank amazingly. Even the slight variations in the current delivered by the microphone would have a powerful effect on the intensity of a glow lamp, especially if the current was amplified.

The rapid flickers of the lamp—so rapid that the human eye could not distinguish them—could be recorded on the sound track, through a slit, as successive, tiny, individual pictures. This kind of sound track looked different from the other: the variations of the light left fine stripes of varying density, or darkness, which suggested the rungs of a ladder. From then on the three men themselves always called it the "rung script," but it is now known as a variable-density sound track.

An old problem—how wide the light slits should be—still remained to be solved. Engl demanded a tenth of a milli-meter. The others flinched at the idea. Would the photo-conductive cell respond to the light getting through a slit that was only about as wide as a hair?

Engl defended his proposal. Their apparatus, if it was not to lose the sibilant sounds of speech and the overtones of music, must respond to, and reproduce, a frequency as high as 6,000 vibrations a second. Experiments in radio broadcasting had proved that. In one second 24 pictures ran through the camera and projector, each one—following Edison's dimensions—19 millimeters high; that is, in each second 456 millimeters of film ran past the slit. If, then, they wanted to capture and reproduce a frequency as high as 6,000 per second, the slit could be only 1/6,000 of 456 millimeters wide. That would be considerably less than a tenth of a millimeter—only 0.076 millimeter, to be exact. "With our present slit, a millimeter wide, we pick up, of course, frequencies no higher than 456 per second—not much higher than the standard A."

"It's enough to drive one crazy," declared Massolle. "With the means at our disposal today we can certainly not meet that requirement."

Vogt, mediating as usual, said: "It's the same old technical problem: to satisfy exaggerated demands as well as we can with the available means. Without meaning to be a prophet, I say the answer might be a slit that is somewhat wider, at first, than a tenth of a millimeter. That means that for the time being we must give up the higher pitches. Perhaps we can console ourselves by remembering that every device has been improved in time."

They experimented and tested, tested and experimented, and sat—with pounding hearts, with anxiety, with confidence —in front of the loudspeaker.

And, even though they were not completely satisfied, the superiority of the new technique was undeniable.

On June 3, 1919, they were granted a patent on the use of the glow lamp for sound films.

Then they amplified the current carrying the sound from the microphone, built machines for the continuous development and printing of the films, and changed the form of the glow lamp. They provided the camera with a sound-proof cover so that its clatter would not drown out the sound that was to be recorded, and they sound-proofed, with hundreds of borrowed potato sacks, the room in which the microphone and camera were set up. For the sound-reproducer they replaced the photoconductive cell with the recently developed photoemissive cell (now called simply photocell or phototube), which responds much more quickly to changes in light; substituted a focused beam of light for the light passing through a narrow slit; and finally developed their own loudspeaker, an electrostatic one called the Statophone, which was tuned for their purposes. They worked with the frenzy that always takes possession of creative men who are obsessed with their mission.

They applied for one patent after another. Each application was the result of a series of experiments, hopefully planned, anxiously carried out, and happily finished—the product of painful work, the result of their rock-like confidence. By 1922 they had applied for about 170 patents. They were granted 107; the National Patent Office had acknowledged, 107 times, that their idea was new, was a step forward.

And then came the day when they could unite all their devices into one great apparatus. The sound vibrations, picked up by the microphone and amplified, were transformed by the glow lamp into variations of brightness, which, on being photographed, produced thin stripes of varying density on the sound track beside the pictures. During reproduction these varying stripes passed through a very strong, focused beam of light, which, more or less weakened by the stripes according to the sound, fell on the photoemissive cell, which transformed the variations of light into variations of electric current, which was amplified and then carried to the loudspeaker.

One point, however, had to be reconsidered. Since the sound track demanded a uniform continuous movement, the pictures a jerky movement, the pictures and the corresponding sound track could not remain beside each other on the strip of film. The three inventors decided to let the sound track run ahead of the corresponding pictures. While the pictures, moved along by the Maltese-cross drive, passed through the projector in jerks, the sound track, twenty frames in advance, passed at the same speed, but smoothly, through the sound apparatus below the projector.

With the help of a few patrons the inventors shot a few short films. *Life in the Village*, with its acoustically promising scenes in a chicken yard, was the longest. On September 17, 1922, at the Alhambra in Berlin, they first presented their art to the public as Tri-Ergon—that is, as the Work of Three.

A Berlin newspaper reported the event: "We see now the first scenes of the 'talking film'. First impression: technically, it is successful. On the screen appears a gentleman who gives a lecture. Every syllable corresponds to the movement of his lips. The mouth opens as the word is heard. There is no falling behind or running ahead in the speech. Between picture and sound there is complete agreement. Second impression, of animals and animal sounds: the crowing of a rooster is astonishing; the bleating of a sheep has a natural sound. Again we have complete agreement between what we see and what we hear. Third impression, of the dramatic scene: the human voice sometimes sounds phonograph-dead, and not just because of the creaking background noise. It does seem that the human voice wastes away in reproduction: it loses its animation, its modulations, and becomes wooden, for it is the little nuances, one might say, that make up the life of the human voice. Why, then, doesn't the same thing happen to the voices of the sheep and the rooster? Apparently because we don't hear their voices with the ears of a sheep or a hen. God knows what chickens make of their own cackling! Conclusion: However striking the results are, we shall not be able to use the talking film for artistic purposes. The film will remain silent, and that is probably good luck for us."

Despite this judgment, UFA, by far the most important German motion-picture company, risked another experiment. It invested half a million marks in a sound studio of its own, and there it produced *The Girl with the Sulphur Matches*. The picture was a complete failure. After only a few days the first publicly exhibited long narrative film with photographically recorded sound had croaked itself to death, as the newspapers matter-of-factly and cynically reported.

The silent film was achieving triumphs with *The Kid, Queen Christina, The Last Laugh,* and *Metropolis*—showing Charlie Chaplin, Greta Garbo, Emil Jannings, and Werner Krauss. The trade papers never tired of warning people against putting more money into such a lost cause as the sound film. The producers of silent films were, perhaps, glad to be persuaded, for the remodeling of the studios would certainly cost a great deal; and, besides, how would they distribute their films to exhibitors who did not have the equipment for showing it? The owners of motion-picture theaters feared that their equipment would become worthless if the sound film made its way, and the financially weakest of them trembled for their existence. And the actors? How many of them must have been worried by the thought that their personalities would not be attractive or forceful if they had to open their mouths before the camera! All those involved agreed on one point: the greatest advantage of the motion picture, not only as a popular art but also as a business, was its internationality, and this would certainly be destroyed by the spoken word, which would be intelligible only to a limited audience. For all participants it seemed desirable that the film remain silent.

The inventors of Tri-Ergon, after their failure in Berlin, were relieved when a Swiss speculator bought their patent rights; at least they could pay their most pressing debts. Their life work, with their rights as inventors, with all their claims on the future, passed to the Tri-Ergon Holding Company of Sankt Gallen.

14.

HOLLYWOOD AND THE COMING OF SOUND

IN 1781, on the western coast of North America, the Spanish had founded the mission station named Pueblo de Nuestra Señora la Reina de los Angeles, or Village of Our Lady the Queen of the Angels. The name might please Spanish taste, but for everyday use it was certainly too long, and people soon found "Los Angeles" enough.

Maria Theresia, who had ruled Austria-Hungary for forty years, had died the year before the mission was founded; Frederick the Great of Prussia was nearing the end of his long reign; and the social conflicts of France were pressing toward a violent resolution. To Europeans, absorbed in their own problems, America seemed far, far away, and its western coast was almost a mythical land, in which Los Angeles was only a tiny speck that seemed likely to be overwhelmed by its luxuriant tropical vegetation.

When California joined the United States of America in 1848, Los Angeles did not have even five thousand inhabitants —fewer than those crowded together in one modest suburb of Paris. Twenty-two years later, in 1870, Los Angeles still had fewer than six thousand inhabitants. By the end of the century, however, there were already a hundred thousand. It had been discovered that Los Angeles was built above a gigantic underground pool of oil; and oil, in the age of the gasoline motor, meant at least as much as the grains of gold in the Sacramento Valley. At the edge of the city—indeed, even between the houses—the derricks shot up like mushrooms out of the ground.

And Hollywood, the forest of holly trees, with its few isolated farms, sleepy and forgotten, among the foothills of the Santa Monica Mountains?

An ambitious speculator, having bought all the available land, cut it up into building lots and began a gigantic advertising campaign. He boasted of the "most alluring spot on the earth, where sea and mountains kiss each other under an eternally blue sky, where the most luxuriant vegetation thrives in the unbelievably pure air." Villas—built cheaply of wooden frame and stucco, materials well suited to the climate —rose on some of the lots. In 1910, nevertheless, Hollywood was still an insignificant garden suburb of Los Angeles.

In the next year the Hollywood we know was discovered.

For several years the pioneer motion-picture producers of the country—most of them located near New York—had been sending their production units to southern California during the winter. It did not take them long to discover that Hollywood, the garden city between sea and mountains, not only had an incredible number of days of picture-taking weather every year but was within sight of the most various and magnificent scenery that any producer could desire.

Many men discovered, suddenly, that they had a passionate interest in motion pictures. Many simply reckoned coolly that the movie business earned more profit than any other. Everywhere one heard the story of the man in the garment business who noticed the long line of people waiting to get into a nickelodeon, as the first American motion-picture theaters were called. After counting the people who handed in their nickels at the ticket booth every day, he sold his garment business and set out for southern California. He was followed by many, not only from the garment business but from other occupations also, who were attracted to the movies by nothing except the desire to get rich. Among them and their employees, of course, were also some men of imagination and ability, such as David Wark Griffith, Mack Sennett, and Charles Chaplin.

Hollywood was transformed almost overnight. An English journalist reported to his European readers: "The atmosphere of the studios scattered everywhere between gardens and villas—the photographic ateliers, along with their auxiliary installations, are called studios here—seems to seep through the cracks of their walls. Nothing seems natural any more, neither the vegetation—for the leaves of the cactuses and aloes look like painted metal—nor the sky, whose eternally deep blue reminds one of a lowered backdrop; and the wonderful colours of the sunset seem like a clever lighting effect. Even the buildings look like theatre sets: frail wooden frames covered with plaster and papier-mâché, which gives an impression of unreality; behind the facades you expect to see iron props. The people, too, are stagy: the women with excessive make-up, the men often in costume. Numerous Negroes, Orientals, and Indians strengthen the impression of a legendary wonderland. You look over to the flat roof of a cinema theatre and see there an Arabian in turban and burnous, rifle on shoulder, marching gravely back and forth. You hear talk only of films, everywhere and in the most various languages. You move in a world of decorations, theatre sets, projectors, make-up, and celluloid; you become impregnated, surfeited, with it, and at last everyday life seems to be a poor imitation of a photograph. Everything is pleasant; everything seems ready to be photographed the very next minute; everything is neat, pretty, and sweet, but—frankly— without a soul."

In Europe people shrugged. Probably this was all just one of those magnificent promotional stunts in which the Americans excelled. Who cared about Hollywood? In 1912 ninety percent of all the films in the world were still produced in France, and the only others that counted were the grandiose Italian spectacles and the Danish and Swedish human-interest films.

Then Europe tumbled into the madness of World War I.

The rulers of American movies rubbed their hands with satisfaction. The war meant big business for them. The American market, for which, until now, they had struggled painfully with the French, fell into their hands overnight; the French had other things to take care of than turning cellulose into films. And the American market meant a great deal, for the Americans were undoubtedly the most devoted moviegoers in the world—a fact on which learned men were seriously pondering.

The learned men found an explanation: The American people, who for more than a century had devoted all their strength to the conquest of their country, who had led, or had had to lead, a hard and strict life, suddenly found themselves facing an entirely new situation. A well-ordered life now gave them leisure; advancing industrialization shortened their working hours; they had become prosperous. They lacked only one thing: the knowledge, derived from experience, of what a person could do with his free time.

The movies solved their problem.

People filled the movie theaters and the purses of the movie kings. And when the war in Europe came to an end, Hollywood's magnates not only controlled the American market but were well prepared to conquer the untended European market. American films soon flooded Europe.

Hardly ten years after the First World War, 1,250,000 people lived in Los Angeles. Every year, out of a thousand wells, flowed oil worth $200,000,000.

The suburb of Hollywood had 140,000 inhabitants. Ninety percent of the world's films were made in America, and three-fourths of those were made in the sixty big studios of

Hollywood. Gaumont of Paris, the most venerable film company, had stopped production; the English, Scandinavian, and Italian producing companies were dead; and the German UFA, America's only competitor, passed into American hands. In America alone the movie industry skimmed off annual profits of more than two billion dollars. Every foot of exported film made a profit of a dollar, and millions of feet of film were exported.

Hollywood, for the whole world, had become a concept: it was the source of mass entertainment.

In the middle of the 1920's the attendance at movie theaters suddenly dropped considerably, especially in America. Perhaps the decline was simply a harbinger of the world economic crisis that began in 1929—the possibility of which no one was willing to admit; perhaps moviegoers were simply getting bored. The movie companies saw only that their business was threatened, that their shares were falling on the stock market. Many feared complete ruin, among them one of the biggest, Warner Brothers.

In desperation Warner Brothers risked all they had in one gamble. They would win back their old public, which seemed to be tired of movies, with something new: sound pictures, or, as they were called at first, talkies.

A number of men had been trying for years to combine the phonograph and the motion picture. Oskar Messter, in Germany, used a mechanical method of amplifying the sound of phonograph records for the sound films that he made in 1903 and 1904. Léon Gaumont, who had begun experimenting in 1901, gave public performance of his *film parlant* (talking film) in Paris in 1913 and then demonstrated it in the United States. A German combination of phonograph and motion picture, called the Synchroscope, was demonstrated successfully in this country but was soon abandoned because not enough pictures with sound had been made to supply the theaters in which the system was tried. Edison, in 1913, returned to the problem of combining the phono-graph and the motion picture, and he too (this was before electronic amplification was generally available) used a me-chanical method of amplifying the phonographic sound; amplification for a large audience was necessary, for Edi-son's new talking pictures, unlike his peep-show Kinetoscope, were projected. His program of talking pictures ran for several months at a theater in New York and was shown in other American cities and in other countries.

Lee De Forest, the American inventor of the amplifying tube called the Audion, had been working on the photograph-ic recording of sound and by 1923 had achieved results sim-ilar to those of Engl, Vogt, and Massolle. He had produced a few films with sound and had persuaded a few theaters to install the equipment required for showing them; but his system, called Phonofilm, failed to arouse any enthusiasm in the big motion-picture producers, perhaps because his films, like Edison's films with phonographic sound, seemed too much like mere demonstrations of a new technique: they did not use sound to move an audience by expressing human emotions.

De Forest—and, in fact, most of the experts—believed that sound would be useful in educational films, newsreels, travel films, and others in which sound effects and a com-mentator's voice were added to what began as a silent film, but that narrative or dramatic films in which the whole story was told by recorded dialogue would never replace the silent films. Like the inventors of Tri-Ergon, De Forest had to sell his rights in the system he had developed.

Despite all these experiments and demonstrations, films with sound had not been commercially successful, and no big motion-picture producer had been convinced that they ever would be. D. W. Griffith, generally considered America's best director, used phonographic sound in 1921 for a scene in a picture called *Dream Street*, but this was soon forgotten. Few theaters were equipped to show such films, and it was therefore a real gamble when Warner Brothers, with the courage of despair, acquired the right to use Western Electric's system of film with phonographic sound. This system, named Vitaphone, had electronic amplification and a new type of loudspeaker.

Warner Brothers' first program of Vitaphone pictures was presented in August 1926. The camera and the turntable on which the extra-large records had been cut had been driven by the same motor; they were synchronized well enough so that the producers dared, in the short pictures, to record dialogue as well as singing; but the feature, entitled *Don Juan* and starring John Barrymore, had only orchestral music and sound effects. The program aroused no excitement, probably because the pictures, like Edison's earlier attempts, were regarded as mere novelties and failed to move their audiences. But Warner Brothers were encouraged to try again, and with *The Jazz Singer*, presented to the public in October 1927, they made history.

The Jazz Singer, which is now remembered as the film that introduced the era of sound pictures, was really made, almost entirely, as a silent picture, with the dialogue and explanatory narrative given in subtitles. The star, Al Jolson, spoke only a few lines of dialogue and sang several songs; but those songs, added to an appealing story, were enough: audiences, forgetting about the technical innovation, were moved. They clamored for more.

The outlook changed overnight. The newspapers fanned the flames of excitement. Warner Brothers shares rose from 22 to 140 dollars. A sound-film frenzy gripped the world—especially Hollywood.

The phonographic system of sound used in the first Vitaphone pictures had hardly achieved its worldwide success when it was displaced by a better system.

William Fox, one of the most powerful men of the movie industry, on a trip to Europe, had stopped at Sankt Gallen, in Switzerland, and had acquired, for a trifle, the rights of the Tri-Ergon Holding Company.

In secrecy, with his staff of technicians, he had discussed and compared several of the most promising photographic systems: the Tri-Ergon system, the Photographophone system of Ernst Ruhmer of Berlin, and the system developed in America by Theodore W. Case, who had collaborated with De Forest for several years and then had begun to work on his own. Case's system was similar, in principle, to the Tri-Ergon system but was able to use some improved devices that had been developed since 1919. In 1926 the Fox Film Corporation purchased Case's system, to which it gave the name Movietone, and it soon organized Movietone News for the production and release of newsreels. The first public showing took place in January 1927, nine months before the release of *The Jazz Singer*. Although these factual shorts did not move audiences as *The Jazz Singer* moved them, it soon became obvious that the photographic sound track was greatly superior to the phonographic record. Even Warner Brothers admitted this and abandoned the system they had recently introduced.

During all the years when inventors were struggling to develop phonographic and photographic recording of sound for motion pictures, the basis of a better system had already been discovered and was waiting to be improved.

Valdemar Poulsen of Denmark, in 1898, had discovered that sound could be recorded magnetically on wires, disks, or tapes of a suitable material. He called his invention the Telegraphone, and it was used in an office dictating machine that was put on the market in this country about 1917. In that same year an American magazine mentioned the possibility of using a stripe of powdered iron on motion-picture film for the recording and reproduction of synchronized sound. It was more than thirty years before this principle was put to use.

15.

WHAT THE SOUND PICTURE NEEDS IS A GENIUS

"AM I in your way, Mr. Fürlinger?"

"Not at all, Miss Herta; just stay where you are. It will be some time before I get around there." The old man, as he went on brushing the plush-covered benches along the walls of the waiting room, kept muttering about his penny-pinching employer, who, after the last showing had begun, always turned off all the waiting-room lights except the weak bulb in the ceiling.

"Oh!" groaned the girl. "I simply can't sit still. I'm too excited."

"You should have watched the picture," said the old man, going on with his brushing without looking up. "There were plenty of seats. Now that unemployment has got so much worse, even here in Vienna, the higher-priced seats are always empty; people simply can't afford them. It would have been a distraction for you."

"Really, Mr. Fürlinger!" protested Herta. "You are now showing *The Blue Angel* for the third week. It's bad enough to see a picture a second time and always know what's going

to happen, but twenty times?—even though I am fond of
Emil Jannings and Marlene Dietrich. I already know every
single one of the 170,000 frames—that's how many run
through the projector in two hours, Peter says."

"Peter has to watch it three times a day—and four times
on Sundays and holidays!"

"But that's all part of his job! Who worries about me
when I have to stitch up two hundred blouses exactly alike?"

She stood up and tripped nervously round the showcase,
in which eight glossy prints showed scenes from *The Blue
Angel*—with the strange result that she suddenly asked: "Do
you know, Mr. Fürlinger, how many photographs are made
all over the world every year?"

The old man, of course, did not know.

"Forty billion, says Peter—forty thousand million!"

Fürlinger, not startled by the figure, responded in his own
way. "Thanks for reminding me that I must change those
pictures today. A new program begins tomorrow—an American film, *All Quiet on the Western Front*. You will certainly see it . . ."

"That's tomorrow, Mr. Fürlinger, tomorrow! What good
does it do me today, when I'm so excited? He was at the
Patent Office today!"

"Who? Peter?" He even stopped brushing.

"Yes, with his invention. Hasn't he ever told you about
it? He has invented something that will let you see the
pictures on the screen in three dimensions." She suddenly
felt the need to talk about what was on her mind. "It's not
something simple that you look at through red-green glasses.
No, it's done with prisms. Narrow prisms, turned alternately
to the right and to the left, run up and down the whole
screen; one group throws a picture into the left eye, the
other a slightly different picture into the right eye. It needs
a projector with two objectives, of course. He has already
sketched it for me any number of times—but I can't say I
really understand it completely."

"Soooooo . . . !" The O was long drawn out, but Herta failed to hear any tone of happy surprise.

"But you mustn't give anything away, Mr. Fürlinger. Peter might not like it if he knew that I've told you about it—although he says that nothing can upset it once he has applied for the patent." She spoke solemnly: "It is protected from the day of application."

"No, no, I won't spill anything."

He brought out the placard for the next picture and then, planting himself in front of the girl, asked: "And what will the result be—for the movie business, I mean? What will happen then?"

"Oh, nothing special. All the movie theaters will be re-modeled, Peter will get his share from all of them, and we can finally get married."

Fürlinger remained standing there. He unrolled the plac-ard and rolled it up again. He felt obliged to explain him-self. "You see, I'm a little worried about these technical novelties. Before they really do any good, a lot of people have to suffer for them. That began long ago with the weavers, and it was the same when the sound film came in. In the papers you could read how everybody was worried about what would happen to the stars, to the directors, to everybody in the movie industry—except the musicians. No-body worried about the musicians. But think of what hap-pened to Peter's father. Old Horak had been playing the piano here in the Aurora Cinema ever since the Krause Cinema, in the Prater, burned down. He had a steady, well-paid job. And overnight the sound film destroyed his liveli-hood—his and thousands of others."

The old man had to stop for breath. It was probably the longest speech he had made for many years. He leaned on the rolled-up placard.

"I had worked here with Mr. Horak for a long time. The thing hit him very hard. Peter had to drop out of the Technical High School. It was lucky for him that he had hung around here since he was a child and could get the job as projectionist. But you know all about that." He picked up the roll again and laid it across his shoulder. "That's why I'm a little suspicious of all these technical novelties."

"Oh, you needn't worry about Peter's patent."

More than six months had passed. *Bombs on Monte Carlo* was running at the Aurora Cinema, and a young woman sitting in the last row was following it, in utter boredom, for the tenth time, as she waited for her Peter. Since her working hours ended after his had begun, there was no other way for them to exchange a few words. This was not the kind of life she had wanted.

As the last chords died away and THE END faded from the screen, Herta strolled past Fürlinger, who was bowing out the customers, and into the waiting room. At last Peter came down and hung up his key in the little office. He gave old Fürlinger an affectionate slap on the back, as usual, but the youthful laughter was missing from his glance.

Quietly they went two blocks to the coffee-house where they had already ended many a day. There, without a word, Peter passed a sheet of paper across the table. Herta's eyes flew over it: "Austrian Patent Office . . . First Preliminary Decision . . . The preliminary examination, carried out according to section 55 of the Patent Law, has produced the following result. You are requested to respond to this Preliminary Decision within two months after receiving it . . ."

The back of the sheet was covered with typewriting. She read something about a Dr. Herbert Ives, in America, who seemed to be working along the same line as Peter. But Peter's hand covered that and pointed to the following paragraph:

"It would therefore first be necessary, on further presentation of the application, either to explain thoroughly, with respect to its optics, the consequences of the proposed arrangement or to present convincing evidence of its practicality."

This was followed by the impression of a rubber stamp and by a signature.

She handed the paper back to him. A shiver ran over her; thinking the cold marble tabletop was the cause, she slid a newspaper under her bare elbows.

"And I've always thought that as soon as you put in your application . . ."

Peter smiled for the first time that evening.

"And won't you get any money now?"

"I shall have to sit down and write out a still more detailed description, so that the man can visualize everything. It would be better, of course, if I could demonstrate my projection screen, just as I have imagined it, with a double projector . . . but . . . do I have the money for that?"

Herta pouted sullenly. It was all different from what she had imagined. Was this what was going to get them out of the rut they were in?

"I'll simply have to show drawings."

He had already taken out his pencil and gone to work on the margin of the newspaper that lay under her arm. Oh, these lines were all familiar to her, however little she understood them. And now he would begin with his angles of reflection . . .

Her glance wandered listlessly over the paper. Suddenly it stopped. "King Kodak is dead!" The boldface letters caught her attention, and she read on. King Kodak, some American multimillionaire or other, had shot himself during the afternoon of March 14, 1932.

Her thoughts tumbled over one another: that was yesterday, yesterday afternoon, just as she was running blouses through the sewing machine and was figuring, for the thousandth time, how a movie projectionist and his young wife could get along if the wife contributed her meager seamstress's wages to the common household expenses. And for the thousandth time she had come to the conclusion that they wouldn't do at all badly if . . . and then came the obstacles, which lay like heavy boulders in their way: they had neither home nor furniture, Peter had to help his parents, and her mother, no longer eligible for the dole, would also need help.

Yes, she had been thinking about all that yesterday, and at the same time an American worth millions of dollars had shot himself!

The whole story seemed so strange to her that she suddenly had to turn the newspaper round, though Peter was far from the end of his troublesome construction of angles and his exposition of the relations of light beams.

She broke into his eloquent explanation. "Do you know of a King Kodak?"

"Of course! That's what they call George Eastman. Every month, in Rochester, New York, he produces 10,000 miles of film—every year enough to go five times round the earth! He uses up 10,000 tons of cotton for it, and a third of the silver produced in America."

Peter simply knew everything!

"Then read this."

Together they read about King Kodak, who, a perfect example of the self-made man, had risen from a poverty-stricken youth to become a symbol of affluence, who had later given away million after million because, to the end of his days, the memory of his early poverty oppressed him. In both America and Europe, for example, he had established dental clinics in schools because he was still tortured by the recollection that he had once been unable to pay his dentist's bill. At fifty he began to try to recover what he first had missed and then had sacrificed to his success in life. He learned to dance; he took long vacations; he left himself plenty of time for fishing. It's not known whether these late little pleasures really compensated him for what he had lost, for he had no one to confide in. He had no wife, no family, no children. We know only how much, in his old age, he wished he had a son. At seventy-six he was attacked by an insidious illness. After two years of torment, which neither the physicians nor his millions could alleviate, he threw life off. "My work is done. Why wait?" are supposed to have been his last words.

Months passed again.

Then came the Second Preliminary Decision from the Patent Office. The back of the sheet was again closely written: ". . . Proof of an effect justifying the granting of a patent is now, as before, not given. In case the applicant is not in a position to demonstrate unquestionable advantages on a theoretical basis, there remains the possibility of presenting experimental results. If, however, no further relevant proofs of the advance made by the object which it is desired to patent can be presented, proposal of a motion for the rejection of the application must be reckoned with . . ."

Peter could answer within two months.

This time he too seemed to be at a loss. His blond forelock swayed disconsolately above the marble slab, and the despondent Herta tried in vain to catch his eye. The waiter, yawning, leaned on the coffee-house bar and counted the minutes before closing time. Stale cigarette smoke drifted through the desolate room. Sometimes everything seems flat and hopeless.

"I think I'll look up my old teacher, Burckhardt. He knows his way around in these affairs."

Herta took up the idea eagerly. She would have taken up anything that offered some hope of a way out. "Yes, of course, he should be able to advise you." Then she remembered: "Oh, he was the one that always called you Scamp?"

"Yes, he was a really fine fellow."

Burckhardt's study was still dominated by a disorder that Peter remembered from earlier days. A mercury-vapor lamp and two cathode-ray tubes barely held their ground among a great variety of materials—even Danube flint. Everyone know that Burckhardt still had ambitions as an inventor and that he was now searching for an especially luminous material for a television screen; for some day, he was convinced, television would become a reality.

The teacher leaned back in his armchair slowly and comfortably, as if he wanted to gain time. He had greeted his visitor as Mr. Horak, not as Scamp, and he had grown plumper, older, and wearier, but his glance was still bright. And this glance now wandered from the Second Preliminary Decision of the Patent Office over a high pile of books and manuscripts to his young vistor.

Should he tell Horak bluntly what he thought? The young man's eyes looked at him too trustingly.

Burckhardt began, as if he were addressing a class, by going back: the surest way, he had found, of bringing his students to the goal.

"You see, Mr. Horak, after instantaneous photography on film had become possible, Edison's Kinetoscope, the Lumières' Cinematograph camera, and Messter's projector with the Maltese cross were bound to come together to put something usable on its feet—or, rather, on its tripod. I am willing to bet you that Edison was annoyed with himself to the end of his life because he himself had not decided at once to project the pictures onto the wall. And it has been clear from the beginning to every perceptive person that some day, in some form, sound would have to be added. Well, it was added very soon. It often happens that even the experts are right. Today, of course, many people are complaining because the sound film still lacks color. We who work in the field, we know that color not only is

coming but is really already here. Among the various processes I expect the most from those of AGFA and Eastman
Kodak. Why? Because they are being developed by the
largest firms. We agree, certainly, on one thing: solution of
the great problems requires great resources. In Germany—
so I hear, at least—a grandiose color film based on the Baron
Munchausen tales is already being planned."

The young projectionist felt the good will behind the
words, but he couldn't make out how his old teacher was
trying to help him.

"Well, Mr. Horak, the sound film, even without color, has
developed by this time into a fine and respectable fellow.
It's the acknowledged favorite of humanity and is, of course,
pampered and spoiled. It has become a tyrant. It tells us
how we are to conceive of a hero and a villain, of a perfected heart-befuddler and an ideally beautiful woman. It
also, it is true, shows us what is desirable and what is des-
picable, what is right and what is wrong. The constant
flattery in the daily papers, the circulation figures of the
fan magazines, the ridiculous worship of the stars—these
and many other things tell us how firmly it forms and rules
our hearts and our minds. Yes, it's amazing how often
children bring up their parents!"

Peter fidgeted nervously in his chair. Was this why he
had come? Was this his old teacher, who had always had
both feet on the ground?

Burckhardt seemed to guess his thoughts. "And now
you come along, Mr. Horak, and want to make motion
pictures three-dimensional! I ask you, however, whether
the sound picture really needs the third dimension. Many
maintain that what it needs is, rather, a genius who would
make a work of art of it, an enrichment of life, not a mere
means of distraction."

"You are trying to console me, sir," said Peter softly.

"To console you, I could mention other things. Dr. Herbert Ives—the son, by the way, of the pioneer of color pho-

tography—is not your only competitor. The Russians are said to be far ahead of us in this work. Don't forget that other paths could lead to the goal. Don't forget the unlucky gamble on phonographic sound. I have heard of a three-dimensional film that was recently demonstrated to some financiers; instead of red and green light it uses differently polarized light. That too is a possibility. All these processes, including yours, seem to me much too complicated and too expensive. In technology the simplest thing has always won—no matter how much trouble it was to find it. New technical achievements will necessarily become harder and harder and will often be possible only through collaboration. Before the first film with photographic sound appeared, three thousand patents contributing to it, directly or indirectly, had been granted in Germany alone. Before the first colored motion picture, or even before the first really successful color photography, ten thousand patents may be necessary. For a satisfactory three-dimensional motion picture the number could easily be a hundred thousand!"

Now Peter looked his teacher firmly in the eye. He began to understand.

"So don't be unhappy now, Mr. Horak, if your first child is not viable, does not develop at once into a giant. I've gone through all that myself. At the first idea of one's own, at the first application for a patent, one always imagines that the world lies open before one. And remember, when Edison died last year, he had been awarded 1,097 patents in the United States. His famous notebooks—2,500 of them, each with 300 pages—certainly contained ideas for many more. And how many of all those inventions have become as significant as the few we know best—the incandescent lamp, the microphone, the phonograph, and—the Kinetoscope?"

Burckhardt had stood up, driven by his thoughts, and now his broad-shouldered figure moved over to the window.

Peter blinked after him. The man was no doubt right, he told himself. He had finally realized what the teacher wished to tell him. He didn't know, however, whether the agitated girl who was waiting for him down at the entrance would understand all this. And that was why he looked so despairingly around the room.

Suddenly a strong hand seized him by the forelock, as if he were still sitting in the second row at school. "Don't be unhappy, Scamp! Not everyone can win the prize; even very great men have often been losers. You are young and ambitious, and you will have other ideas. And, even if you shouldn't grasp the laurels the next time, I still have a consolation for you: your life will have been filled with a task, it will have had a meaning. Is that nothing? There's always only one victor. It's the same as in the Olympic Games: for everyone the greatest pride is—to have been there and taken part."

EPILOGUE
by the Translator

Peter Horak's former teacher, Burckhardt, was half right in his prediction about the development of motion pictures in color. Four different color processes are in general use today, and two of them are those that he mentioned. The Eastman process and one that Burckhardt did not foresee, Technicolor, are used by all the big motion-picture producers of the United States; the AGFA process and Gevacolor are used in Europe.

The Technicolor process uses three strips of film (one for each of the primary colors), which must be exposed at the same time in a special camera. The Eastman, AGFA, and Geva processes, in different ways, get all three colors on one strip of film, which is coated with three emulsions separated by color filters. There are a few other processes, but they are used only by small producers for special purposes. Every process is very complicated.

One innovation that Burckhardt did not foresee was the projection of motion pictures onto wider screens. Since such screens are usually curved, with their concave sides facing the audience, they give the spectator the feeling of being a part of the scene. If the screen is very wide and sharply curved, and especially if the picture is accompanied by stereophonic sound coming from a number of loudspeakers surrounding him, the spectator may feel that he is right in the middle of the action. He is said to be *engulfed* by the picture, and the process is known as *engulfment*.

The old screen, with which generations of moviegoers had been familiar, was about a third again as wide as it was high; if, for example, a screen was eighteen feet high, it was about twenty-four feet wide. There are four methods of increasing the width in relation to the height.

The method called wide-screen projection uses standard 35-millimeter film with frames (the individual pictures) of the old standard size, but the projector masks a strip at the top and a strip at the bottom of each frame, thus changing the proportions of the picture, and it increases the magnification so that the picture fills a somewhat wider screen.

The second method also uses standard 35-millimeter film, but the frames are made wider, in effect, by an optical trick. A special kind of camera lens, called anamorphic, doubles the camera's horizontal angle of view (takes twice as wide a picture) but squeezes the image (distorts it in a regular way) into the width of the old standard frame. When the film is projected, another special lens unsqueezes the image (restores the proportions of the original scene) so that it fills a very wide screen. The best-known application of this method is called CinemaScope. The principle of the anamorphic lens has been known for a hundred years.

The third method uses film that is 70 millimeters wide, twice as wide as the standard film, with frames of the normal height. The screen is, of course, about twice as wide as high.

The fourth method exposes two or more strips of film with a camera having two or more lenses and exhibits the picture with two or more projectors, each illuminating only part of the very wide screen. In Cinerama, the best-known application of this method, the camera exposes three strips

of film with three lenses separated by angles of 48 degrees.
The lens at the right takes the left third of the scene, the
lens in the middle the middle third of the scene, and the lens
at the left the right third of the scene. The film used is of
the standard width, 35 millimeters, but the frames, instead
of being four perforations high (see the illustration on page
235), are six perforations high. The exhibiting theater must
have three projectors, separated, like the camera lenses, by
angles of 48 degrees, to throw the three pictures, slightly
overlapping, onto the screen, which is very large, sharply
curved, and about twice as wide as high. Although the effec-
tiveness of the process depends to a considerable degree on
the spectator's position in the theater, his feeling of being in
the middle of the action is very strong; if he is sitting in
the area where the effect is strongest, he may even be
alarmed by his engulfment in the action.

The wide-screen pictures and methods of projection, in
varying degrees, give the spectator some illusion of depth,
of three dimensions, but they are not truly stereoscopic;
they are merely panoramic. True stereoscopy results only
when two pictures of the same scene are taken at the same
time by lenses about two and a half inches apart (the normal
distance between the pupils of our eyes) and are then exhibited to us in such a way that the right eye sees only the
picture taken with the right lens, the left eye the picture
taken with the left lens. Our brain then fuses the two pictures into one that seems to be three-dimensional, just as it
fuses the two different images formed by our two eyes.
Stereoscopic still photographs have been known since 1849.

It was not very difficult to design and build a motion-
picture camera that would take stereoscopic pictures, and
young Peter Horak was not concerned with that problem.
He was trying to work out a way of *projecting* such pictures, and that is a really difficult problem.

A motion-picture engineer tells me that a new attempt
to make stereoscopic, or 3D (for three-dimensional), motion

pictures is heard of about every ten years; and many stereoscopic systems have been theoretically worked out. Only
three of these, so far, have had any practical success.

The first method, called anaglyphic, exposes two films
at the same time in a stereoscopic camera. When the film
is exhibited, two filters of complementary colors (usually
red and blue-green) are put in front of the projector lenses,
and both films are projected together onto the screen, one
forming a red image and the other a blue-green image. Let
us say that the projector has a red filter at the left lens and
a blue-green filter at the right lens. Then, if the spectator
wears a red glass before his left eye and a blue-green glass
before his right eye, his left eye will see the image projected
by the left lens of the projector, his right eye the image projected by the right lens, and the two images will fuse into one
that seems black-and-white and three-dimensional. The anaglyphic method of stereoscopy was invented in 1858, long
before motion pictures on film were thought of, and was
first applied to motion pictures in 1897. It cannot be used,
of course, for color films.

The second stereoscopic method separates the two images, not by filters of complementary colors, but by screens
that polarize differently the light from the two lenses of
the projector. If the spectator wears similar polarizing screens
before his eyes, each eye will see only the image intended
for it, and the two images will fuse stereoscopically. A
patent for such a system was issued in England in 1898,
but the system was not practical until cheap polarizing
materials became available in 1932. Stereoscopic motion pictures employing polarization were exhibited in 1939 at the
World's Fair in New York.

The third stereoscopic method separates the two images,
not at the spectator's eyes, but at the screen. One kind of
screen has an elaborate structure of vertical wires in front
of it; such a system was reported from the Soviet Union
early in the 1950's. Another kind of screen is molded so

that its surface is broken up into fine vertical channels (if concave) or bulges (if convex), which seem to be similar to the vertical prisms that young Horak was planning. The wires or channels or bulges are intended to separate the two images thrown by the projector, sending one to the right eye, the other to the left. These screens make it unnecessary for the spectator to wear colored glasses or polarizing screens, but they are very expensive, and the stereoscopic effect is observed only at certain positions in the theater.

None of the stereoscopic systems tried so far has been commercially successful. Inventors will, no doubt, keep trying, even though many people repeat Burckhardt's question: Does the sound picture really need the third dimension?

The latest talk is of a system in which the two separate images will be photographed on the same strip of film, one image on one side and the other image on the other side, with polarizing screens embedded in the film. Perhaps this will confirm Burckhardt's dictum that the simplest thing always wins.

INDEX

with notes, definitions, and illustrations

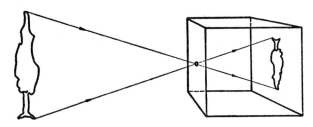

Diagram of a simple camera obscura, or pinhole camera.

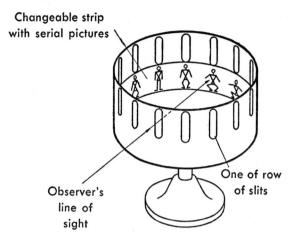

Changeable strip with serial pictures

Observer's line of sight

One of row of slits

Horner's Magic Drum, later known as the zoetrope.

development of television, the sending of photographs by wire, and the development of stereoscopic motion pictures. He was the son of Frederick E. Ives.

Jannings, Emil (1887–1950), 187, 197
• German-Swiss actor who worked for a few years (1926–1929) in American motion pictures.

Janssen, P. J. C. (1824–1907), 98
• French astronomer who began early to use photography in his work: he invented a "photographic revolver" with which he took serial pictures (1874) of the transit of Venus (the passage of the planet Venus across the face of the sun), and he photographed the sun (1877), the great comet of 1881, and sun spots (1885).

Janssen, Zacharias (dates unknown), 12
• Dutch spectacles-maker who built a successful compound microscope about 1590.

Jazz Singer, The, 194, 195
Jolson, Al (1886–1950), 194
• American singer and entertainer.

Kepler, Johannes (1571–1630), 12
• German mathematician and astronomer; founder of modern optics. He discovered the three laws of planetary motion and the inverse-square law stated by Hauslaab in Chapter 4 (that the brightness of light is inversely proportional to the square of the distance from its source). He used a large camera obscura in his work: a revolving tent with a lens in a tube at the top.

Kid, The, 187
Kinetograph, 156
• Edison's name for his early motion-picture camera, and Oskar Messter's name for his motion-picture system (including both camera and projector).

Kinetophone, 127

• The popular name, for centuries, of what we now call a slide projector. It was first described (1646) and demonstrated, perhaps was invented, by Athanasius Kircher, a German priest who was living in Rome as a professor of mathematics. Even in his first demonstration of the apparatus, he projected pictures of the Devil to shock the spectators, just as the phantasmagoria operators of Vienna did nearly two hundred years later. His projector, improved and modified, is one of the essential elements of the motion picture.

• The drive patented by Oskar Messter (German patent No. 127, 913) was a refined and perfected form of earlier devices, one of which, the Geneva stop, was used—for a different purpose—in watches. It is still used in 35-millimeter projectors and in the Moviola, a small, motor-driven film-viewing apparatus used in the editing and cutting of films.

• French physiologist and inventor, one of the pioneers of motion-picture photography and of the scientific film. He invented a number of special cameras for scientific purposes: his "photographic rifle" (1882), developed to photograph the flight of birds, was the first practical portable motion-picture camera; his slow-motion camera of 1894 took 700 pictures a second.

• Ruler (1740–1780) of Austria and Hungary.

• Pioneer Austrian photographer; published, in German, a manual of photography (1846); first president of the Photographic Society of Vienna, founded in 1861.

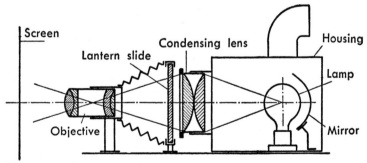

Diagram of a magic lantern (in use the screen is, of course, much farther away than it is here).

Diagram of Messter's Maltese-cross drive: (a) Maltese cross mounted on the shaft of the film-driving sprocket; (b) the circling peg that pushes the Maltese cross through a quarter turn; (c) the cut-away disk that holds the cross fixed when it is not being turned by the peg. The peg and the cut-away disk are both mounted on a wheel that was driven by a hand crank in early cameras and is driven by a motor in present cameras.

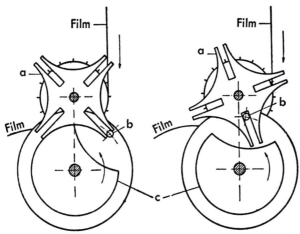

lished in eleven volumes in 1887 under the title *Animal Locomotion*. Muybridge exhibited his motion pictures at the Chicago World's Fair of 1893. He never tried to develop a motion-picture camera, but continued to use rows of many cameras.

Natterer, Johann (1821–1900) and Josef (1819–1862), 69, 81

• Austrian daguerreotypists who shortened the exposure time by sensitizing their plates with bromine and chlorine as well as iodine.

negatives, made by Talbot, 79; positives from, 81–82, 86; glass plates for, 83; Eastman and, 108, 109
New Photographic Company (NPC), 160

• The initials were really NPG, for the company's name, in German, was Neue Photographische Gesellschaft.

Newton, Sir Isaac (1642–1727), 18

• English mathematician and natural philosopher, one of the greatest of all scientists. He is probably best known for the law of gravitation, but he wrote on optics and developed the theory of light mentioned by Ettingshausen in Chapter 1.

New York *Herald*, editor of, 127
nickelodeon, 189
Niepce, Isidore (1805–1868), 36, 43–45, 46
Niepce, J. Nicéphore (1765–1833), 82; early life of, 35–36; and lithography, 36, 37; and heliography, 37–38; and Daguerre, 41–43

• French inventor. Although Niepce made the first permanent photograph (1822), his process could not have led very far, for it required exposures of ten or twelve hours even to produce mere silhouettes of objects against the bright sky. The long exposures were not a serious handicap to the process he called heliogravure, the production of printing plates by sunlight and etching with acid, which is similar, in principle, to modern photomechanical methods of reproduction. He was the first to use the iris diaphragm and the folding bellows in a camera. He and his brother Claude patented (as early as 1807!) an internal-combustion engine that was used in boats on the Seine.

Niepce de Saint-Victor, C. F. A. (1805–1870), experiments of, 82–83, 86, 89

• French physicist (and relative of J. N. Niepce). His albumen-coated glass plates were slow but produced fine-grained negatives of high quality.

objective, experiments on, 52, 53–59, 81; Uchatius and, 68, 71, 72; and mist pictures, 76; for three-dimensional photography, 173, 197

• A lens, or combination of lenses, that forms an image of the object being observed, photographed, or projected. (Some optical instruments—a compound microscope, for example—have another lens, called the eyepiece, through which one looks at the image formed by the objective.)

Oersted, H. C. (1777–1851), 114–115

• Danish physicist, founder of the science of electromagnetism.

Ohm, G. S. (1787–1854), 115

• German physicist, known especially for his investigations of electricity. The unit of electrical

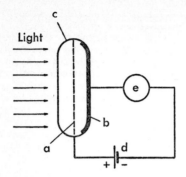

Light

c

e

b

a

d

+ ‖ −

Diagram illustrating the principle of the photoemissive cell: (a) an open-meshed anode; (b) the cathode—a layer of a photoemissive element (the metal cesium, for example); (c) the glass bulb, evacuated or filled with an inert gas; (d) a battery or other source of direct current; (e) a meter that shows the flow of current. The cathode, when struck by light passing through the anode, emits electrons, which are drawn to the anode because it is positively charged; their movement constitutes a current. In practical use the meter is replaced by an amplifier and the device that is to be controlled by the cell.

Science Museum, 79
Scientific American, 95, 119, 123
screen, dimensions of, 207–209
Seebeck, T. J. (1770–1831), 46

• German physicist. In 1810 he wrote to Goethe, who was a friend of his, that silver chloride, under certain conditions, took on the color of the light to which it was exposed. The result was due to the interference of light waves, and it led, eighty years later, to Lippmann's interference method of color photography.

Séguier, Baron Pierre Armand (1803–1876), 69

• Frenchman who introduced the camera tripod, the tent as a portable darkroom, and, in 1840, a compact, light, portable camera with a folding bellows. This camera was much lighter and smaller than Daguerre's, but the daguerreotypist who wanted to use it as a portable camera had to carry also some iodine, some mercury (which is very heavy), boxes in which the plate could be exposed to the vapors of iodine and mercury, small dishes, an alcohol burner (to heat the mercury), and other accessories.

selenium, properties of, 180
Senebier, Jean (1742–1809), 46

• Swiss clergyman, librarian, chemist, and biologist. In 1782 he published an account of his numerous experiments on the sensitivity of various substances (including silver chloride) to light of various colors.

Senefelder, Alois (1771–1834), 36

• German inventor of lithography.

Sennett, Mack (1880–1960), 190

• Canadian-born pioneer Hollywood motion-picture director and producer who specialized in slapstick comedy. A number of famous directors and actors got their start under him. His real name was Michael Sinnott.

serial pictures, 95–96, 98, 101; experiments with, 123–125, 145; *see also* moving pictures

• Pictures showing successive instants in a movement or process. When such pictures are viewed quickly, one after another, our persistence of vision makes the movement seem continuous.

shells, artillery, picture of trajectory of, 70, 74
Siemens, Werner von (1816–1892), 98

• German electrical engineer and inventor.

Siemens & Halske, 142

• German company that manufactured electrical equipment and carried out projects in electrical engineering; founded in Berlin in 1847 by Werner von Siemens and J. G. Halske.

silver, for metal plates, 42, 44, 68, 81; *see also* silver iodide
silver bromide, for plates, 86, 107; *see also* silver salts
silver chloride, experiments with, 78, 79, 81, 82; *see also* silver salts
silver iodide, sensitivity of, to light, 42–43, 44–45, 81; and gelatin, 90–91; *see also* silver salts
silver nitrate, solution of, for prints, 65, 78, 79, 81; *see also* silver salts
silver salts, sensitivity of, to light, 46, 78, 83, 86, 180; dissolving of, 79; *see also names of*
Skladanowsky, Max (1863–1939) and Emil (dates unknown), 131

• German inventors, the first to project motion pictures in Germany (November 1, 1895). Their system (using two projectors) soon fell into disuse.

is a photographic track in which the variations of light produced by the variations of the sound being recorded are registered as variations in the density of the silver deposit produced by exposure and development. The variations in density appear as stripes of varying darkness across the width of the track. In the other kind of photographic sound track, the variable-area track, the variations of light produced by the variations of sound are registered as variations in the position of the boundary between the exposed and unexposed parts (opaque and transparent in the negative) of the track; this boundary appears as a wavy line along the length of the sound track.

Standard motion-picture film, showing two frames: left, silent film (dimensions established by Edison); right, early sound film, with a variable-density sound track.

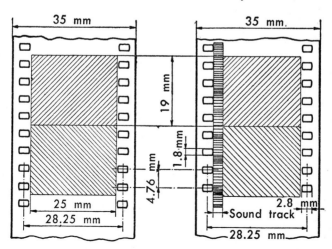

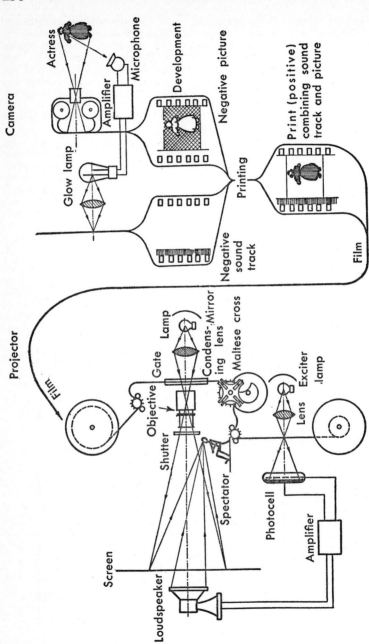

Diagram illustrating the production and exhibition of a motion picture with a variable-density sound track.

Laboratory model of Stampfer's Stroboscope.

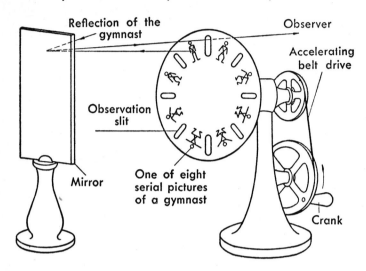

Reflection of the gymnast

Observer

Accelerating belt drive

Observation slit

Mirror

One of eight serial pictures of a gymnast

Crank

Diagram of Uchatius's first motion-picture projector.

PRINTED IN U.S.A.